Children of Poverty

Studies and Dissertations on
the Effects of Single Parenthood,
the Feminization of Poverty,
and Homelessness

Stuart Bruchey
UNIVERSITY OF MAINE
General Editor

A Garland Series

Social Welfare and the Feminization of Poverty

Shirley A. Lord

Garland Publishing, Inc.
New York & London
1993

Copyright © 1993 by Shirley A. Lord
All rights reserved

Library of Congress Cataloging-in-Publication Data

Lord, Shirley A., 1946–
    Social welfare and the feminization of poverty / Shirley A. Lord.
        p.   cm. — (Children of poverty)
    Includes bibliographical references and index.
    ISBN 0–8153–1119–2 (alk. paper)
    1. Poor women—United States. 2. Public welfare—United States.
3. Sex discrimination against women—United States. I. Title. II. Series.
HV1445.L65   1993
362.83'08'6942—dc20   92–33245
                                                                                            CIP

Printed on acid-free, 250-year-life paper
Manufactured in the United States of America

CONTENTS

LIST OF TABLES — vii

ACKNOWLEDGMENTS — ix

ABSTRACT — xi

CHAPTER

1. WOMEN AND POVERTY — 1

2. FEMINIST THEORY AND INEQUALITY — 4

   Liberal, Radical, and Socialist Feminism — 4
   Socialist Feminism and the Sexual Division of
     Labor in the Household — 9
   Capitalist Patriarchy and the Labor Market — 14

3. HISTORICAL ANALYSIS OF SOCIAL WELFARE POLICY
   PLANNING AND IMPLEMENTATION: A FEMINIST
   PERSPECTIVE — 17

   The Elizabethan Poor Laws — 17
   Charity Organization Society and Settlement
     House Movements — 19
   Mothers' Pensions — 22
   The Great Depression and the Social Security Act — 24
   Escalation of Female Poverty: 1940-1960 — 27
   The War on Poverty and the Economic
     Opportunity Act — 32
   The Legacy of Reaganomics — 35

4. POVERTY AS A MEANS OF DOMINATION	38
Statistical Overview of the Feminization of Poverty	38
5. THE POLITICAL STRUCTURE'S RESPONSE: THE AMERICAN SOCIAL WELFARE SYSTEM	48
Social Welfare Policy Issues	48
Social Welfare Programs and Trends in Expenditures	56
6. WOMEN AND THE WELFARE STATE	61
Welfare Reform	61
A Progressive Feminist Social Welfare Agenda	65
7. STRATEGIES FOR SOCIAL CHANGE	77
BIBLIOGRAPHY	80
APPENDIX	91
INDEX	93

LIST OF TABLES

TABLE		Page
1	Percent of Families Below the Poverty Level: 1990, 1985, and 1983	41
2	Number of Families Below the Poverty Line: 1990, 1985, and 1983	42
3	Number of Female Householder Families Below the Poverty Level and Poverty Rate: 1990 and 1959	44
4	Number of Children Below the Poverty Level by Race of Family Head: 1990, 1973, and 1965	46
5	Federal Outlays for Human Resource Programs: 1966-1992	54
6	Federal Expenditures for Major Human Resource Programs Fiscal Year 1988	57

ACKNOWLEDGMENTS

This revised dissertation represents my ongoing interest in and research on feminist theory and inequality. I was fortunate to study with two scholars who challenged me to grow intellectually and encouraged me to develop a political awareness of feminist issues.

I am extremely grateful for the direction and guidance given to me by Ben Agger, Chair of my dissertation committee, and Beth Anne Shelton, committee member. Professionally, they are committed to the highest standards of teaching and scholarship. Working with them has made me a more critical writer and a better teacher.

The community at Buffalo State College, where I teach in the undergraduate Social Work Department, fosters a learning environment in which scholarship is encouraged and supported. I will forever be grateful for the sabbatical I was granted to complete my dissertation. Barbara Sirvis, my former Dean and current Vice President for Academic Affairs at SUNY College at Brockport, supported my interest in feminist issues and showed by her accomplishments that women can achieve their full potential if given equal opportunities. Ellen Kennedy, Chairperson, Social Work Department, shared her knowledge and expertise on poverty and provided critical feedback. My colleagues listened patiently to my ideas and helped clarify my thinking. The students, who participated in my classes each semester and openly debated contrasting points of view on women and welfare, provided intellectual stimulation and continual encouragement.

The love of my mother, Agnes; brother, Ron; and sisters, Donna, Pat, and Janice, is a constant source of strength and reassurance. I am grateful to my friends who help me keep a balanced perspective on my work and help me maintain my sense of humor.

I am especially grateful to Nancy Heyer for her computer expertise, constant encouragement, and endless patience. This accomplishment is shared with her and Tom.

I dedicate this dissertation to impoverished women whose daily struggles are testimony to the resiliency and dignity of the human spirit.

ABSTRACT

This study addresses sexism within the American capitalist patriarchal system and the repercussions of discrimination on women within the household and in the labor market. The study is broadened to analyze the sexist subtext of the American social welfare system and its impact on poor women and their children.

Capitalism justifies job segregation by sex and a domestic division of labor in the home. The relationship between women's subservient position in the household and their secondary status in the labor force is parasitically interdependent. Because women are in disadvantaged economic positions in home and work environments, they are at high risk for becoming poor should their spouses die, desert, divorce, or separate. Forced into the competitive labor market, they are hired in low paying, unstable, unfulfilling jobs with high rates of unemployment and underemployment. They frequently end up as recipients of Aid to Families with Dependent Children (AFDC), the welfare program for single women with children, receiving benefits below the national poverty level. This "new" social problem is labeled the "feminization of poverty" and refers to the growing percentage of poor who are women with dependent children.

Historical analysis is used to study the problem of the pauperization of women. The task of feminist theorizing is incomplete. Feminism runs the risk of becoming a single issue theory and practice that only relates to white, middle-class women. The feminist perspective needs to be further universalized to include a broad social problems focus. Social welfare policy, which establishes guidelines for the public social welfare system, is analyzed from a historical perspective within the feminist theoretical framework of socialist feminism.

A progressive feminist social welfare agenda is proposed that impacts on poor women and their children.
The goal is elimination of poverty not reformation of the welfare system because the majority of poor are not on welfare. A progressive feminist agenda identifies structural barriers that cause poverty rather than blames individual deficiencies. The agenda proposes progressive

economic, family, and health care social welfare policies that produce long-term systemic change. Proposals include strategies for full employment, comparable worth, parents' wages, tax reform, minimum income guarantee, children's allowances, child care services, and universal health care.

Strategies for implementing a progressive feminist social welfare agenda are discussed.

WOMEN AND POVERTY

The message of capitalism is oftentimes intolerance for those who do not or cannot achieve in the American class system. While profits of political and corporate leaders continue to rise in the current fiscal environment of the early 1990s, economic and political resources of the poor, unemployed, underemployed, homeless, women, elderly, inconvenienced, and working class continue to erode. Throughout this period, some liberals have come forth and articulated concern for the plight of the destitute and impoverished. Liberals speak about modifying or reforming capitalism, but "their views do not entail a fundamental critique of capitalism itself, or lead to visions of or programs for a socialist society" (Galper 1975, p. 18). The desire of liberals to reformulate existing policies and reform current legislation are constructive activities; however, serious efforts at social change require the reconceptualization and restructuring of capitalism. The outcome would be reduced profits and privileges for white males who currently control political and economic power in America. Both men and women need to be educated about the complexities of the existing patriarchal capitalist system before movements toward a more democratic socialist form of governance can be proposed with any reasonable hope for change.

In this theoretical study, I historically analyze the American social welfare system and its relationship to the rising trend in female poverty. I begin by reviewing current sociological literature on feminist theory and inequality. I address the issue of patriarchy within the American capitalistic system and its repercussions on women's work both within the labor market and the household. I suggest that the current configuration of patriarchal capitalism is accepted uncritically and supported unconsciously.

My argument is that the capitalist patriarchal system justifies job segregation by sex and a domestic division of labor in the home. This relationship between women's subservient position in the household and their secondary status in the labor force is parasitically interdependent. Because women are in disadvantaged economic positions in both home and work environments, they are at high risk for becoming poor should their spouse die, desert, divorce, or separate. Forced into the competitive labor market, they are hired in low paying, unstable, and unfulfilling jobs with high rates of unemployment and underemployment. They end up frequently as recipients of public welfare receiving benefits below the national poverty level.

A discussion of the historical response of social welfare policy planners to women and poverty shows how the cycle of poverty for women often unfolds gradually and subtly. Homemaking, child care, and housekeeping are necessary tasks within a family that are usually assigned to women. When mothers work at home, capitalism does not define those tasks as productive labor, so they receive no economic remuneration. Because household work is not worth money, it is not valued and, in reality, not even counted as work. In capitalism, where money and profit determine worth, women and their work in the home are not valued. This not only impacts on women at home but also in the market place when they attempt to find jobs. Household responsibilities impact negatively on job opportunities and wages for women. They are categorized as less reliable and more risky due to the fact that they have the primary responsibility for maintaining the household and rearing children.

When husbands leave for a variety of reasons, women are then forced into the competitive labor market in order to support dependent children. Having sole responsibility for care of the children is one of the major factors in the feminization of poverty. Data collected on poverty trends in America indicate that the fastest growing type of family is that headed by a single woman (Rodgers 1986; Sidel 1986; Kamerman & Kahn 1988). Thus begins the decline of single-parent families into poverty. Female-headed families tend to be poor due to factors related to underemployment, unemployment, and welfare benefits that are below adequate subsistence levels. This is what is meant by the concept of the "feminization of poverty."

Analysis of the feminization of poverty reveals that public policies have not kept pace with private issues. Social welfare policy has not historically and does not currently reflect the changing role of women in society. The Equal Rights Amendment has floundered as a political agenda. Women continue to struggle for wage equality and equality of opportunity in the labor market. They are rarely offered the same employment opportunities and chances for advancement as men; when women are in comparable positions to male counterparts, they are often paid less for the same work. The majority of working women are in low paying, low-skilled service jobs with inadequate and costly day care alternatives for their children. Increasingly large numbers of women are ending up as recipients of the welfare program predominated by female family heads and their dependents, Aid to Families with

Dependent Children (AFDC).

Feminist scholars and sociologists need to devote more attention to the study and assessment of increasing rates of poverty among women. In addition, escalating rates of unemployment and underemployment for women need to be analyzed. Not until the 1970s were women even included in studies on the job market and household labor. These women tended to be white, middle-class subjects; poor women have historically been excluded from analyses. Sociology also needs to focus more attention on the nation's failure to adapt its social policy to the changing role of women. This study will contribute to the new and growing body of theoretical literature on capitalist patriarchy and its relationship to women and inequality.

I begin with the basic tenet that institutional discrimination against women and sexist socialization remain entrenched in the American culture. Change strategies that focus more on structures than individuals need to be emphasized if the problem of the feminization of poverty is going to be addressed effectively. Liberal reforms may assuage temporarily the symptoms of the problem, but only radical changes in the sexist way that American capitalist patriarchy deals with women of all income levels and races are going to eliminate the complex problem of women and poverty.

FEMINIST THEORY AND INEQUALITY

Liberal, Radical, and Socialist Feminism

Feminist scholars are gaining recognition as influential voices for social change in the midst of current economic, social, and political class struggles. Feminist theory is an intellectual orientation as well as a social movement that addresses unequal gender roles. Feminist theory addresses the impact of oppression on women. Economically, women are oppressed because they provide cheap or completely unpaid labor in the home. Sexually, women are oppressed in terms of the biological imperatives of reproduction along with the assignment of the role of primary care giver for children. Finally, women are responsible for the socialization and moral education of children.

The roots of women's oppression and strategies for social change are analyzed from three separate schools of thought within the feminist theoretical framework. They include liberal, radical, and socialist feminism.

For liberal feminism, sexism is basically the blockage of women's career paths as well as exclusion of women from the labor market. Liberal feminists do not advocate fundamental restructuring of the social order but believe that gender inequality can be addressed within the confines of the present political, legal, and capitalist economic systems. Because liberal feminists are concerned with status attainment, social change is measured by the extent to which individual women rise up through the political, economic, and social hierarchies of society. The liberal feminist school views sexism from an individual perspective rather than from a group or class perspective.

Because liberal feminism focuses on the individual, it believes that sexual exploitation can be eliminated by using the power of reason to gain mutual cooperation between men and women. Liberal feminist scholars present critiques of traditional patriarchal family roles, sexist hiring practices, pay inequity for women, affirmative action, comparable worth, lack of federal support for day care, and inflexible maternity leave policies (Jaggar 1983; Donovan 1985). Liberal feminists believe optimistically that the state will eventually intervene on behalf of women's rights.

Liberal feminists support the division between the realm of the public and the realm of the private. In the public sphere, their goal is an androgynous society where women have equal opportunity to work alongside men for equal pay and benefits. In the private sphere, they want a companionate marriage or a marriage in which both husband and wife equally share household and childrearing responsibilities. Critics argue that this liberal theoretical approach reinforces a sexual division of labor in the labor market and in the household. The public sphere of work and politics, which is dominated by males, takes on more importance than the private sphere of childbearing, childrearing, and housework, which is predominantly performed by females. The male sphere of production, therefore, becomes more critical than the female sphere of reproduction.

Another intellectual tradition within feminist theory is radical feminism. It critiques the notion of a patriarchal society in which men have all the power and use it to dominate women. Whereas liberal feminism focuses on unequal rights and lack of opportunities to explain women's oppression, radical feminism emphasizes male domination of women as the problem. Radical feminism is not so interested in the public realm of economic issues of production but rather in the private realm of the processes of reproduction. Radical feminists analyze the ways in which sexist American culture reproduces itself. A crucial contribution to radical feminist theory is Chodorow's (1978) The Reproduction of Mothering: Psychoanalysis and the Sociology of Gender. She uses a Freudian perspective to analyze how young males and females are socialized differently. She discusses in detail the relationship between sexist socialization and the sexual division of labor.

Radical feminists argue for a women's perspective on culture. Gender is the critical issue more than race or class. They criticize compulsory heterosexuality as the cornerstone of women's oppression. Radical feminists are not exclusively lesbians; however, they do view lesbianism in larger political terms. Sexuality is not simply personal choice or biological determinism but is a larger sociopolitical set of social relations and political processes. Radical feminists emphasize that the biological makeup of women is used to exploit them as reproducers of children and objects of sexual gratification and voyeurism. The personal is defined as political because private oppression impacts on the sexist ways that women are treated in the political and cultural spheres.

Radical feminists articulate strong views on patriarchal family life and culture. Greer (1971) asserts that "Women's liberation, if it abolishes the patriarchal family, will abolish a necessary substructure of the authoritarian state, and once that withers away Marx will have come true willy-nilly, so let's get on with it" (p. 326). Millett (1970) argues that a "sexual revolution would bring the institution of patriarchy to an end, abolishing both the ideology of male supremacy and the traditional socialization by which it is upheld in matters of status, role, and temperament" (p. 62). In discussing revolutionary alternatives to the current patriarchal structure, Firestone (1970) demands "the freeing of women from the tyranny of their reproductive biology by every means available, and the diffusion of the childbearing and childrearing role to the society as a whole, men as well as women" (p. 233). Atkinson (1974) envisions women organizing as a power block and exhorts women not to get married for their "own sake as well as for the Movement's" (p. 105).

The radical feminist school is criticized for its strong emphasis on the private and personal realm of women's oppression. Some refer to its focus on the social relations of reproduction as biological determinism, while others question its lack of attention to the public or political nature of women's oppression. Radical feminists do not trust or believe in the inherent goodness of the state; the state is simply an extension of the patriarchal family structure. Radical feminism supports the creation of alternative women's structures, programs, institutions, and services.

Development of a feminist theoretical perspective is at an embryonic stage, and precautions must be taken against concentrating on issues that only relate to white, middle-class women. The perspective needs to be further universalized to include a broad social problems focus particularly as regards the causes and outcomes of oppression of poor women. Feminist scholars are beginning to respond to the issues of racism and poverty through the theoretical perspective of socialist feminism.

Socialist feminism incorporates some tenets from liberal feminism although it rejects liberal feminism's assumption that women's equality can be achieved within a liberal capitalist market economy. Socialist feminism also accepts some of radical feminism's basic principles. It accepts radical feminism's critique of compulsory heterosexuality; however, it argues that both liberal and radical feminists need to give greater emphasis to an economic understanding of women's oppression. Socialist feminist analysis is a synthesis of Marxism and feminism. Although the dialogue between Marxism and feminism is sometimes tense, Marxist analysis is integral to the study of women's oppression. Eisenstein (1979a) explains that:

> First, it provides a class analysis necessary for the study of power. Second, it provides a method of analysis which is historical and dialectical....it can also be used to analyze the patriarchal relations governing women's existence and hence women's revolutionary potential. One can do this because Marxist analysis provides the tools for understanding all power relations;... (pp. 6-7)

The women's movement has been critical of Marx and Marxists for their lack of attention to the realm of reproduction although there are signs that Marxists are attempting to rethink the "woman issue." Marx's (1918) theory on economic value that he outlines in Capital is integral to any discussion of the role of women's work in the household versus the labor market or of reproduction versus production. He theorized that commodities have three kinds of values: "use value," "exchange value," and "surplus value." Use value is something useful that "becomes a reality only by use or consumption." Home labor such as cooking, knitting, and weaving produce articles that have use value. Exchange value "presents itself as a quantitative relation, as the proportion in which values in use of one sort are exchanged for those of another sort, a relation constantly changing with time and place." It is here that Marx begins to discuss alienated labor or "human labor in the abstract." Surplus value is "the difference between the value of the products of labor and the cost of producing that labor power, i.e. the laborer's subsistence" (pp. 1-5; 300-311). In other words, the excess worth that the capitalist owner gains as profit from workers' labor power is surplus value.

Marx relegated "women's work" or housework to a marginal status and excluded it from productive labor. This distinction between productive and unproductive labor is critical because it reinforced a historical precedence of viewing productive labor as male waged labor and nonproductive labor as female household labor. Industrial capitalism took men out of their homes and into waged jobs in factories; the majority of women stayed behind in the home to do unpaid housework and perform the sex-stereotyped role of mother. Because they received no wages, women's work was valueless. Productive work was waged labor or labor that produces surplus value known as capital. The reproduction of labor power was not productive labor even if it was socially and industrially necessary. Thus begins the institutionalization of the sexual division of labor in American society organized around maximizing profits for the owners of the means of production.

Socialist feminist theory focuses on the sexual division of labor. Thorough analysis of women's oppression involves a broad critique of the subordination of the private to the public realm, of female to male, of people of color to white Americans, and of non waged valueless household activity to waged "valuable" work in the market place. Socialist feminism examines critically the subordination of the realm of reproduction to production.

Socialist feminist theory emphasizes the dominance of the patriarchal nuclear family. Men dominate and run the family, and a sexual division of labor exists where women are primarily responsible for running the household. Men are responsible for paid work. The business community and two-earner families generally view women's work outside the home as extra income and, therefore, not as valuable as men's work. Socialist feminist literature challenges the notion that the legally sanctioned patriarchal nuclear family is the only acceptable lifestyle.

The socialist feminist perspective integrates the tenets of liberalism, Marxism, and radical feminism. "The emerging synthesis locates the oppression of women in the ways that the power relations of capitalism (class domination) and patriarchy (male domination) together structure ideology, the social relations of gender and class, and the overall organization of society" (Abramovitz 1988, p. 24). Capitalist patriarchy both justifies and reinforces the unpaid labor of women. Supposedly valueless labor is valueless only by reference to standards established by the capitalist market economy. Sexism becomes part of the structure of the capitalist economy producing what some socialist feminists call patriarchal capitalism. You cannot talk about capitalism without including patriarchy; they are intricately and complexly linked.

The most recent studies of gender inequality show that an analysis of capitalist patriarchy must include an analysis of the role of women in the household and how that role affects participation in the labor market (Eisenstein 1979b). Regardless of whether one looks at women's oppression politically, economically, psychologically, or biologically, women experience oppression within the family. Since socialist feminism focuses on the household, let's continue the discussion by looking at the sexual division of labor in the household. The negative impact of the division of labor at home on women's labor market participation is analyzed later in the chapter.

Socialist Feminism and the Sexual Division of Labor in the Household

Data on household labor delineated by gender indicate that married women devote a great deal of time to household labor. Wives devote approximately 30 to 60 hours per week to domestic work; they contribute 70 percent of the total time all household members spend on domestic tasks. Husbands do very little to assist with housework or with care of the children. Husbands devote approximately 10 to 15 hours per week to domestic work; they contribute 15 percent of the total time all household members spend on domestic tasks (Berk 1985).

Socialist feminist writers argue that women function in the private sphere as noncitizens and nonrational beings in order to meet the needs of patriarchy. This is a prime example of when the personal becomes political. Women's biology is used by the patriarchal culture as a mechanism of control. "Because patriarchal ideology presents motherhood as natural, woman's assignment to the private sphere and dismissal from the public realm is argued as a defense of the natural order of things" (Eisenstein 1981, p. 16).

The issue of women and household labor is complex. It is a biological and a social issue, yet it has economic ramifications and political implications. Assigning women primary responsibility for household work is prevalent in American capitalism but has evolved from pre-capitalist times. Structurally there are some differences between capitalist and pre-capitalist modes of production due to the shift of the waged work place from home to highly mechanized and supervised factories. In the pre-capitalist period, the household was the locus of both productive and reproductive activities. Nevertheless, men maintained control over the family. Marriage and property laws during that period supported a private patriarchal system in which husbands had absolute power over their wives and children. The onset of capitalism and industrialization reduced men's power over production by placing them into factories where the owners of the means of production controlled their labor and wages. In the household, however, private patriarchy continued to reign and was reinforced by such policies as the family wage which supposedly provided adequate earnings for men to support their wives who were at home taking care of the household and the children. Hartmann (1981) notes that the family wage itself is "the cornerstone of the present sexual division of labor, the economic cornerstone of the nuclear family, and consequently of women's continued economic dependence on men" (p. 15). How this historic development left women oppressed in the home is a subject given considerable attention by socialist feminist scholars (Mitchell 1971; Sokoloff 1980; Barrett 1980).

Male symbolism, ideology, and imagery dominate American capitalist culture. One of the arenas in which this patriarchy is most clearly played out is in the traditional nuclear family structure. The man/husband/father is the main wage earner whose salary supports the family and whose masculine superiority secures him the right to establish the rules and regulations by which all members of the family abide. This narrow definition of the family serves to reinforce the low status of women and to maintain a mythical image of a traditional family structure that no longer predominates. The next chapter's historical analysis of social welfare policy demonstrates how social policies have repeatedly been planned and implemented to uphold and reinforce the values and principles of the traditional nuclear family. The outcome has been the establishment of a welfare system that discriminates against women who do not follow prescribed codes of moral conduct.

Today's family should be defined more broadly as an aggregate of people who cooperate economically and share a social bond. Social policy should impartially reflect a realistic definition of family as it actually exists and not bestow unequal favors on traditional nuclear families by granting generous tax breaks and paying higher Social Security benefits. In my opinion, a family may include lesbian and gay couples, some of whom are raising children; single parent families in which most are headed by women; childless couples; communal families living cooperatively; welfare mothers with dependent children; and unrelated single people living together.

Benston (1969) was the first socialist feminist to focus attention on the seriousness of housework as an economic issue rather than solely one of biology. Benston saw the labor performed in the household as pre-capitalist survival and stressed that under capitalism it is women who continue to produce use values that are consumed by their immediate family. Because this work is not wage labor, it is not counted. Women's work is valueless because it is not worth money and is, therefore, not even work. This fact is the material basis for the inferior status of women. In a society in which money determines value, women, who perform valueless work, can hardly be expected to be worth as much as men who work for money.

This is an important piece of feminist work because it

combatted the argument of those who claimed that the economic exploitation of women occurred only in the work place. It is also critical because it focused discussion on a new analysis of "reproduction" which included not only biological motherhood but also household work.

One problem with Benston's analysis, pointed out by Malos (1980), was that her characterization of housework as "pre-capitalist" production of "simple use values in these activities associated with home and family" still left household labor, even though "socially necessary," floating in a historical limbo somewhere quite outside the capitalist economy (p. 12). Later feminist writers removed household labor from its limbo and decisively placed it in the realm of productive labor. Dalla Costa and James (1980) argue that "Household labor is productive if one thinks of the enormous quantity of social services which capitalist organization transforms into privatized activity, putting them on the backs of housewifes" (p. 173).

The development of a theoretical body of literature concerning the sexual division of labor in the household is a relatively new perspective in feminist scholarship. Glazer's (1980) work on gender stratification demonstrates how mainstream sociology has for years ignored women's domestic labor and women's position in the social class structure. The emphasis has been on men and men's experiences in the work place. She contends that past research on the effects of domestic work on women has been class-biased and underemphasized. The political and economic implications of women having primary responsibility for work in the home merits a great deal more study. In addition, the issues of comparable worth and wages for household work are two recent proposals that merit further dialogue.

As valuable as theoretical treatises are on the subject of sexual stratification, important empirical studies are also being conducted on domestic labor. Sociology is just beginning to recognize the need for empirical studies on household labor. In fact, in reviewing empirical studies on class, stratification, and work, it is difficult to find research that includes data on women and racial minorities. As legitimate as researchers' claims may be that it is difficult to gather data on women, I suggest another interpretation is that women are a low priority. This is another manifestation of discrimination against women in our culture. Not surprisingly, most of the research on the sexual division of labor is being conducted by female sociologists.

Coverman (1983) explored the relationship between domestic

labor and wage labor by estimating the relative influence of hours spent in domestic labor on women's and men's wages. Her research produced two significant findings. First, results supported the hypothesis that "the time currently married women and men spend in housework and child care exerts a negative influence on their wages". Secondly, Coverman found that "the class structure affects women and men differently due to the organization of domestic production" (p. 634). The implication of her findings for future research is that social scientists must give consideration to the domestic division of labor in analyses of economic inequalities between women and men. By concentrating exclusively on market work, most social research has presented only a one-sided view of the system of gender stratification.

Duncan and Corcoran used Panel Study data which provided information on the work history and labor force attachment of a large, representative sample of working women and men. Like Coverman, Duncan and Corcoran's (1984) findings support the conclusion that household responsibilities impact negatively on women's earnings in the labor market. They found that domestic responsibilities account for only about one-third of the wage gap between men and women. They argue that discrimination and socialization account for the remaining two-thirds of the earnings gap.

Although discrimination and socialization are difficult to quantify, research demonstrates that a scientist's preconceived notions about the role of women can interfere with allegedly objective data analysis. England challenges the recent works of Solomon Polachek who bases his theorizing on the acceptance of the basic fact that women's employment is intermittent because of household responsibilities. He hypothesizes that women who plan intermittent employment will prefer occupations with lower penalties for depreciation, whereas men or women who plan continuous employment will have no reason to avoid jobs with high depreciation risks (Polachek 1979).

England's (1982) research on women and labor force attachment strongly refutes Polachek's contention that women freely choose jobs in the secondary labor market for economic reasons. She found that women who had more continuous employment histories were not more likely to be in predominantly male jobs than women who had sporadic employment histories. Women are penalized for time spent away from work whether in female or male occupations.

An enlightened discussion of capitalist patriarchy and the

sexual division of labor must include domestic labor as well as the labor market. Household labor is a new and relatively unexplored topic in the current literature, and additional research needs to be conducted. Initially, even feminist writers ignored the issue of housework. It wasn't until the early 1970s that socialist feminists began to focus attention on household labor.

In recent years, socialist feminist analysis has been criticized for inadequately addressing the oppression experienced by poor women and women of color. These women did not have the option of staying in their own homes to do domestic work. They worked as slaves, cleaning ladies, pickers, mammies, and in other service sector jobs in order to fulfill capital's need for cheap labor. The patriarchal system gave mixed messages to women depending on their class. Upper- and middle-class white women were supposed to stay home and be responsible for the household; lower- income women were expected to work in the public sphere. Socialist feminism is beginning to incorporate the unique experiences and problems of impoverished women in its analysis of oppression. This study on women and the welfare state is a contribution to that growing body of literature.

The multifaceted restrictions that capitalist patriarchy imposes on women's full and equal participation in the labor market are reinforced in the household. In woman's roles as wife, mother, and housekeeper, she is expected to manage all the household chores and perform all wifely and motherly duties. She receives no pay for services rendered, and the work has no status and fewer positive rewards. In addition, she oftentimes works outside the home, so she has dual work responsibilities to perform both in the labor market and within the home. The relationship between the woman's role in the household and her role in the labor market is explored next.

Capitalist Patriarchy and the Labor Market

Increased interest in the synthesis of Marxist theory of capitalism with socialist feminist thought on male dominance has resulted in an attentiveness to the impact of patriarchy on women's role in the production of use value versus exchange value and the impact of women's household responsibilities on labor market participation. Socialist feminist scholars are identifying one of the central problems in the struggle for economic and political equality as the persistent attachment of women to domestic work.

Although the sexual division of labor existed in pre-capitalist times, patriarchal capitalism intensified the distinction between valued paid work in the public arena and valueless unpaid work in the private arena of the home. Women's work takes on value only when it has exchange value in the public marketplace, and even at that point, its value is relegated to second class status in secondary sector jobs. Studies demonstrate that women's inferior position within both the family and society is not simply biological but rather historical and cultural in nature (Hartmann 1979; Sacks 1979; Kelly 1984).

Man's physical superiority enabled him to hunt, fight, and conquer nature, while woman's purported more fragile nature was amenable to the performance of menial chores and tasks. Major socialist writers such as Marx (1964), Engels (1942), and de Beauvoir (1953) link the confirmation and continuation of women's oppression with the establishment of her physical inferiority for hard manual work.

Rather than accepting the physiological argument for male dominance, socialist feminist authors discuss male supremacy over women in terms of patriarchal ideology. Male supremacy is not due solely to biology but rather to a predominant value system that conditions women to exhibit male-serving behavior and to accept male-serving roles. Millett (1970) asserts that this ideology permeates every aspect of culture and touches every aspect of our lives. "Sexual politics obtains consent through the 'socialization' of both sexes to basic patriarchal polities with regard to temperament, role, and status. As to status, a pervasive assent to the prejudice of male superiority guarantees superior status in the male, inferior in the female" (p. 26).

The superior status of the male in American patriarchal capitalism is most clearly demonstrated in the competitive labor market. Sokoloff (1980) argues that "The modern bureaucratic form of twentieth century United States is not simply organized in a manner to make profits for capital. It is likewise organized to ensure that material benefits accrue to men through the exploitation of women's labor" (p. 236). Thus, capitalist patriarchy entails power relationships in which men socially and economically dominate women.

The relationship between woman's role in the labor market and her role in the household is a relatively new area of research. Socialist feminist scholars view wage inequality as a structural issue, and they are beginning to explore the existence of two distinct labor markets: a primary one into which men are most often recruited and a secondary one into which women are usually hired (Eisenstein 1979a; Sokoloff 1980; Barrett 1980; Berk 1985; Donovan 1985). Women are recruited into the secondary labor market because of real or assumed responsibilities for taking care of children and household tasks. Socialist feminism concludes that socially structured institutional constraints determine women's disadvantaged market position rather than professional qualifications. Changes must occur in discriminatory practices and sexist socialization patterns in order for gender equality to be achieved.

This study of the social welfare state and the feminization of poverty broadens the analysis of the vicious circle of sexist oppression to include women who end up poor as a result of divorce, abandonment, widowhood, or being single parents. One of the critical factors that contributes to the feminization of poverty is the fact that women are deemed primarily responsible for caring for children and not men. When attempts are made by these women to enter the competitive job market, employment prospects are usually restricted to the secondary job market where pay is low and work is unstable and unfulfilling.

A major factor contributing to female poverty rates is that women earn approximately 70% of what men earn, and indications are that this trend is continuing. Gender segregation in the job market persists with certain jobs being designated as "female" and others as "male." Secretaries, nurses, and elementary school teachers are women; corporate executives, physicians, and engineers are men. The more an occupation is associated with women, the lower its average wage level (Hartmann, Roos, & Treiman 1985).

Women continue to earn less than men for comparable work despite Title VII of the Civil Rights Act of 1964, the Equal Pay Act of 1963, and other laws which prohibit sexual discrimination in employment and compensation. Wage inequality and low earnings are primary explanations for women's overrepresentation in state welfare programs. They frequently end up as recipients of public welfare in the means-tested cash assistance category of Aid to Families with Dependent Children (AFDC), receiving benefits below the 1990 national poverty rate of $13,359 for a family of four (U.S. Bureau of the Census 1991).

Sexism is ingrained in our society, and the resulting inequalities are apparent both in the household and in the job market. What is not so apparent in the literature is the effect that capitalist patriarchy and the sexual division of labor have on poor women in the welfare system. Sociologists and feminist scholars have not focused their research efforts on them. Some say that poor women are difficult to identify; others mention that they are unreliable research subjects. I suggest that perhaps looking at these women and their children, struggling in poverty in the wealthiest industrialized nation in the world, is uncomfortable. If we study them, then we have to admit that they do exist and that their numbers are growing. They prove that sexist exploitation and oppression remain in modern day America. They remind feminists that not all sisters have made progress, and they might even embarrass "successful" women who have been integrated into the male-dominated spheres of business and politics.

Women in poverty need to be studied and supported. The growing number of women and children in America who are poor is a national disgrace. Increased attention must be given to their plight, and strategies need to be implemented that eliminate, not merely reduce, their poverty. In addition, the role played by politicians and social welfare policy planners in the pauperization of women needs to be clarified and critiqued. The next section historically traces trends in social welfare policy and analyzes their sexist and racist implications.

HISTORICAL ANALYSIS OF SOCIAL WELFARE POLICY PLANNING AND IMPLEMENTATION: A FEMINIST PERSPECTIVE

Government intervention in social welfare has always been controversial. From the 1600s to the present, the needs of society's poor have been addressed reluctantly and acrimoniously. In the United States, it required the impoverishment of an entire nation during the Great Depression to motivate the federal government to become involved in social welfare programs. In fact, countries of Western Europe were years ahead of the United States in funding and implementing welfare programs for families, children, the aged, and the sick. Gradual expansion of the American welfare state demonstrates several historical trends in the treatment of the poor. They include punishing the poor for being poor, funding and overseeing welfare programs at the local or state level, underbudgeting welfare programs that serve the poor, emphasizing the work ethic, delineating between the deserving and undeserving poor, and categorizing and stigmatizing those who seek welfare services. An outcome of these trends has been the establishment of social welfare policies that are paternalistic and repressive.

The Elizabethan Poor Laws

It is important to begin an analysis of American social welfare policy in England because the social welfare system, established in America in the early 1700s, duplicated the tenets and principles of the English model. The English government passed the first poor law legislation that dealt with the destitute of society. The Elizabethan Poor Laws, which were codified in 1598 and enacted in 1601, remained in effect until the middle of the nineteenth century. They embodied conflicts between the desire to reinforce the feudal system and the increasing assumption by civil government of responsibility for the poor.

The Elizabethan Poor Laws initially established the principle of punishing the poor for being poor. One of the basic governing principles was that the family was ultimately responsible for taking care of its own. Parents had the legal responsibility to support their children and grandchildren. On the other hand, children were also responsible for the care of their needy parents and grandparents. Those individuals who would not work were usually committed to houses of correction, beaten or maimed, or even put to death. There were no mechanisms established by which recipients could protest the violation of their human or legal rights.

The Poor Laws also established the historical pattern of stigmatizing the needy. The Act of Settlement restricted the right of the poor to move freely among the parishes and required paupers to wear the letter "P" on their clothing. They were forced to live and work in deplorable and unsanitary conditions. For these reasons, this period earned the reputation as being harsh and repressive (Webb & Webb 1927).

The Poor Laws firmly established the principle of local responsibility of each parish or locality to support its own indigent. In addition, a pattern of categorizing the needy began with the Poor Laws and remains in effect in the American welfare system. In order to be eligible for benefits, recipients must fit certain prescribed labels such as elderly, disabled, unemployed, mother with dependent children, poor, or blind. This system first began in the 1600s at which time the welfare laws designated three main categories of needy: children, the able-bodied, and the impotent (Trattner 1979).

The ideology of blaming the victim is one of the most deeply ingrained principles of the original Poor Laws that has been passed down through the centuries and is reflected in current social welfare policies. It is more gratifying for social workers to focus their altruistic efforts on reforming deficient individuals than it is to design change strategies that restructure entire political and economic systems. Ryan (1971) refers to blaming the victim as "a brilliant ideology for justifying a perverse form of social action designed to change, not society, but society's victim" (p. 7).

The work ethic repeatedly emerges as a central theme in social welfare history. Usually the emphasis is on finding productive work for men, not for women, unless the women are poor. Lower-class women should work, but middle- and upper-class women's rightful place is presumed to be in the home performing household labor; their domestic work is considered unproductive and is, therefore, unrewarded. Starting with the Elizabethan Poor Laws, all able-bodied poor people, including children, were required to work in workhouses or poorhouses or face harsh punishment. This compulsory work requirement conveniently provided cheap labor for newly developing capitalist enterprises in the colonies. Some form of work requirement is attached to most Aid to Families with Dependent Children (AFDC) programs today. With little education and no training, participants in AFDC workfare programs have a minimal chance of securing jobs that provide wages and benefits adequate to support families which would free them from welfare dependency.

In summary, the English system of welfare blamed victims for causing their own impoverishment. Because the poor were at fault, the English government punished and repressed them. It separated them into distinct categories and then stigmatized and embarrassed them. The government established "local responsibility" for the poor; today this concept is called states rights. Families were ultimately responsible for taking care of their own. When unable to do so, local government punitively supplied as little relief as possible. Restrictions were placed on where the poor could live; today this is called a residence law. Acting on an appeal from Connecticut, residency requirements were declared unconstitutional by the United States Supreme Court in 1969. In 1967, Connecticut's federal court ruled the state's relief residency requirements unconstitutional. The majority of the court held that "the right of interstate travel also encompassed the right to be free of discouragement of interstate movement" (Piven & Cloward 1971, p. 307).

Charity Organization Society and Settlement House Movements

The first private social welfare movement was organized in America by Josephine Shaw Lowell. The Charity Organization Society Movement (COS) originated in England in 1869 and was based on the principles of Spencer's Social Darwinism. Social Darwinists argued that the state's role as a mediator between capital and labor should be diminished. Social problems destroy the healthiness of society. COS opened its first office in the United States in 1877 in Buffalo, New York. Lowell believed that poverty had its roots in the inferior character of the poor. She was convinced that tax-supported relief was not the cure but the cause of pauperism by undermining self-reliance and the will to work. Pauperism could be eliminated through the investigation and study of the character and needs of those seeking help and through attempts to educate and develop the abilities of the poor (Germain & Hartman 1980). Many of Lowell's ideas influenced early social welfare policy and continue to be reflected in current welfare programs and practices.

The vision of society that underlay late nineteenth century and early twentieth century social welfare policy was one in which the fortunes of humankind were determined largely by physical and biological forces that a benevolent and enlightened upper class could attempt to control by social engineering, using many of the new tools of science that were emerging rapidly in that day. Major ideas came from scientists like Francis Galton, Charles Darwin and Herbert Spencer and from political scientists like Adam Smith and Robert LaFollette. Social workers became interested in the newly developing social sciences of the day like sociology, anthropology, and psychology.

The science of eugenics became very popular during this period and had an influence on social welfare policy. Because eugenics contended that the human race could be improved by better breeding, it reduced explanations for poverty, mental retardation, psychiatric disorders, physical inconveniences, and criminal behavior to biological determinism. The next logical step was to develop social welfare policies that guaranteed the isolation and removal of unwanted and undesirable people from society. This was the time in history when large state institutions for the mentally retarded and mentally ill and state prisons were built as far from populated areas as possible. It was also the time that special schools were created to deal with children who were different.

Some examples include: the New England Asylum for the Blind was founded in 1829, Ohio established the first state institution for the blind in 1837, and Dorothea Dix began an investigation of the care of the insane in 1841. Robert Hartley, a charity worker, organized the New York Association for Improving the Condition of the Poor in 1843. In 1850, Massachusetts incorporated a school for the idiotic and feebleminded youth, and in 1878, Josephine Shaw Lowell successfully campaigned for New York to become the first state to create a school for feebleminded girls (Alexander & Weber 1978).

A serious implication of this preoccupation with eugenics became evident for women when sterilization was approved in the early 1900s. In 1927, the United States Supreme Court, in the Buck versus Bell case, declared that sterilization was constitutional (Katz 1986). With the approval of the nation's highest court, designated welfare officials had the authority to determine poor and troubled women's reproductive futures.

The antithesis of the micro interventionist approach of blaming the individual's genetic structure or moral decay for social problems was occurring in Germany under the leadership of Karl Marx and

Friedrich Engels. In 1848, they published The Communist Manifesto, a radical ideological treatise that exhorted the poor, the laborers, and the disenfranchised of society to unite and revolt (Marx and Engels 1966).

Because of Marx and Engels, socialism ceased to be merely a form of idle speculation for philosophers given to utopian fantasies. Socialism became a political movement embracing millions of people. "Their radical antithesis was a penetrating analysis of the causes of social inequality combined with a political program of action designed to speed the birth of a new and more equitable social order" (Lenski 1966, p. 11).

The writings of Marx and Engels impacted on the newly developing field of social work. One of their most significant contributions was to focus on the structural causes of inequality, poverty, and basic lack of freedom of people rather than to blame people's individualistic moral deficiencies or sociobiological inferiorities. This was revolutionary thinking especially when compared to the eugenics movement.

In the late 1800s, a group of social workers, who were called settlement house workers, began to broaden the focus of the one-on-one casework approach of working with the poor to macro social work which intervened to change the political and economic systems. They were mostly college educated women from middle-class backgrounds who lived among poor immigrants and migrants in settlement houses that became the core of social, cultural, and political activities for the neighborhood. One of the most prominent settlement workers was Jane Addams who established Hull House in Chicago in 1889. Like Marx, Jane Addams' focus on the structural causes of inequality was revolutionary in the area of philanthropy and not widely accepted. She became known as a progressive seeking social justice and social control. Just as Marxism was stirring controversy in Europe, Jane Addams and other feminists were criticized for the radical nature of their social, political, and legal reforms.

Residents of settlement houses became champions of social reform. Living among the poorest classes of industrial workers and immigrants, they recognized the damage done by unsanitary housing conditions, overcrowded flats, low wages, and night work for women and children. From the settlement houses came the call for slum clearance, for special juvenile courts to deal with young offenders, and for the organization of the Consumer's League to help the housewife and to protect the health of the family. They requested housing legislation, supported better health care programs, and advocated for child labor laws. They worked for the reform of municipal governments, woman suffrage, the rights of women and men in industry, and the problems and exploitation of immigrants. They became involved in the Peace Movement as World War I approached.

I offer an observation on social work's hesitancy to get involved in the macro political arena of systemic change. Social workers were predominantly charity workers who were middle-aged, upper-class, white females. Jane Addams and other settlement workers were atypical. The charity workers were raised in the cultural milieu of the late 1800s that said a woman's place is in the home or in the community doing charitable works of mercy. They believed that nurturing and caring were inherited female traits that came natural to women. Hesitancy to enter the competitive political world of labor unions and government in order to affect social change reflects the sexist philosophy of that historical time with roots both within the psyche of the female social workers themselves and within the male-dominated economic and political structures.

Mothers' Pensions

By the early 1900s, the focus of social welfare planning and policy making had shifted from establishing programs and services that separated families to ones that attempted to keep them together in their homes. In 1909, President Theodore Roosevelt convened the first White House Conference on Children to deal with the growing problem of dependent children. Its major recommendations were to establish a federal children's agency and to strive to preserve the traditional family unit. The recorded Proceedings (1909) stated that "Children of worthy parents or deserving mothers should, as a rule, be kept with their parents at home" (p. 6). How "worthy" or "deserving" were defined was left to the discretion of local welfare officials. Their decisions often reflected racist, sexist, and moralistic attitudes toward minorities and women.

In 1911, Missouri and Illinois passed the first mothers' pension legislation. By 1931, every state except Georgia and South Carolina had instituted mothers' pensions. Pensions had strict eligibility requirements and went to only a fraction of potential recipients. In most cases, the women had to be widowed; divorced women were usually ineligible. There were residency requirements and strict moral codes of behavior that were to be followed by these women. At this point in history, the state became very involved in monitoring the private relations between parents and their children.

On one level, mothers' pensions helped some women and their children stay together through difficult financial times. Closer analysis, however, reveals the very roots of the sexist subtext of American social welfare policy. The pension program was based on the assumption that it was women's responsibility to stay home and take care of the children. In order to be eligible, however, these women had to be widowed which is a condition that is not their fault. In contrast, divorced women, who are at fault for not keeping their marriages together, were ineligible for mothers' pensions. This was the beginning of social welfare policies that reflected traditional moral standards and made distinctions between deserving and undeserving recipients.

Mothers' pensions were the forerunners of AFDC benefits. The main eligibility standard was the "suitability" of the home of the applicant. This was a vague standard that enabled local officials to subjectively interpret policy. "They tended to restrict the programs to nice Anglo-Saxon widows and to move separately but in concert to protect their young programs from Negro and unmarried mothers who might well attract criticism" (Bell 1965, p. 19).

Approval of the mothers' pension program is a critical point in social welfare history because it marks the beginning of the institutionalization of the powerlessness of poor women. It is beneficial to men to have women stay home and take care of the household because that reduces the competition for jobs in the labor market. In addition, placing women in unpaid household positions guarantees that men's domestic needs will be met at no cost to them.

The initiation of a mothers' pension policy also had implications for children. Social scientists and politicians expounded the social and psychological benefits of keeping children with their own families. The reality was that institutionalization was simply not solving children's problems, and the costs of maintaining staff and buildings were becoming increasingly prohibitive. With the initiation of mothers' pensions, women became responsible for childrearing and housekeeping at a cost effective rate. Keeping children in their homes saved capitalists money and spared social workers and psychologists the embarrassment of explaining why their treatment modalities were not producing desired outcomes.

The years between World War I and the Depression of the 1930s were peaceful and prosperous. Social work's involvement in radical reform movements waned because of the war and the impact of the Russian Revolution. Social work became more conservative and more interested in Freud's psychoanalytic theories of personality than in Marx's radical treatises on revolution. Once again social welfare policy began addressing the individualistic intrapsychic causes of poverty rather than the structural issues such as sexism and racism that prevent large groups of people from competing equally in the labor market.

The Great Depression and the Social Security Act

The Depression of the 1930s resulted in a major transformation in the way in which society viewed unemployment and poverty in America. These problems could no longer be viewed solely as moral deficiencies of individuals because the wealthy were standing in bread lines next to the poor. In 1934, Franklin Delano Roosevelt appointed a cabinet Committee on Economic Security. The chairperson was Frances Perkins, the Secretary of Labor. She was the first woman cabinet member and a social worker. As a result of the Committee's report, Congress passed the Social Security Act of 1935 which committed the nation to a program of unemployment and old age insurance and public assistance to the poor. The Social Security Act marked dramatic changes in the principles and practices of the American social welfare institution. For the first time in American history, the federal government assumed responsibility for social welfare programs. This Act was the high point of social welfare policy implementation during the New Deal.

The Social Security Act outlined two major types of programs: the social insurances which are contributory and the public assistances which are outright grants to the poor. More than any other nation, America makes clear distinctions between the benefits of social insurance programs, which are based on work experience and available to all regardless of income level, and the benefits of public assistance programs which are means-tested and go to the poor.

The social insurances, which were based on a joint employee-employer contributory scheme, provided for old age insurance and unemployment insurance. These programs were instituted during the Depression to appease the growing dissidence between unemployed male workers and corporate leaders. The federal government successfully used the strategy of increasing spending on welfare programs to quell civil unrest and temporarily quiet the masses. A similar tactic was employed by President Lyndon Johnson to calm the urban and racial unrest of the 1960s.

Today, the social insurance programs, which include Social Security and Unemployment Compensation, have expanded to become the largest and most costly programs in the welfare system. Rather than hearing a public outcry about the spiraling costs of the social insurances, these programs enjoy the strong support of both business and labor. Some analysts assert that corporate leaders support the social insurances because they keep the workers happy and do not cost the employers additional money. Workers pay both direct and indirect taxes to the social security system that amount to over 10 percent of their income. As of 1991, workers are taxed at the rate of 7.65 percent of the first $53,400 they earn each year, and employers are taxed at the same rate. Many employers escape the costs of paying social security taxes by shifting the cost to the workers in the form of lower wages (Katznelson & Kesselman 1987).

When established during the Depression, income maintenance or public assistance programs were "grants-in-aid" programs which set up a partnership between the states and federal government. The programs in this category were grants for the needy aged, dependent mothers with children, crippled children, the blind, and federal monies for state and local public health work. The federal government set up the regulatory policies, the states administered them, and funding was provided on a matching federal-state basis. Whereas the social insurance programs were federally administered and mandatory, the public assistance programs were administered at the state level, and decisions regarding whether or not to implement the programs were left to the discretion of local officials.

The American tenet emerges once again of rewarding those who work and are worthy of benefits in contrast to making it as difficult as possible for those who are poor and unworthy. Included in the category of undeserving were women with dependent children. At its inception, Aid to Dependent Children (ADC) was thought to be a temporary transitional program; however, it has grown to become the largest public assistance program due to the escalating numbers of poor women and children.

Despite the relative acceptance and popularity of mothers' pensions, Aid to Dependent Children received little attention in 1934 during the Committee on Economic Security hearings. The Committee described mothers' pensions as measures "designed to release from the wage-earning role the person whose natural function is to give her children the physical and affectionate guardianship necessary not alone to keep them from falling into social misfortune, but more affirmatively to make them citizens capable of contributing to society" (Report of the Committee on Economic Security 1935, p. 36).

Although the majority of social workers in the 1930s were women and the Chairperson of the Committee on Economic Security that established welfare program priorities was a woman, the program aimed at alleviating poverty among women and their children received the least attention at the hearings. On the other hand, the programs that were work-related received the most support and highest level of federal funding. These were the programs that predominantly affected white males in the labor market. The most highly educated and professional women of that era accepted the capitalist patriarchal ideology that not only is a woman's "natural" function to be at home with children but also that her role in the household is less important than the economic security of working men in the competitive labor market.

Additional New Deal policies reinforced discrimination against women. It was widely accepted that married women should leave their jobs to permit unemployed men to work. Large numbers of women lost their jobs in 1932 when the federal government ruled that husbands and wives could not both hold federal positions. Officials directing the Civilian Works Administration (CWA) and the Works Progress Administration (WPA) automatically gave men priority over women in work relief programs. The National Recovery Administration (NRA) instituted lower wages for women than for men in identical positions. Female heads of households received no personal benefits under the ADC program, and widows did not receive the Social Security benefits of their deceased husbands. Labor unions systematically excluded women from leadership roles and negotiated labor contracts that paid women lower wages then men (Ware 1981).

The impact of accepting this sexist ideology in the 1930s is still being felt in the 1990s by women and children struggling to meet stringent public assistance eligibility standards and survive on meager benefits. The lack of attention given Aid to Dependent Children in the 1930s resulted in its being administered under the same umbrella as the adult category programs. Because of this, the states had to go through cumbersome bureaucratic processes in order to receive federal approval to administer ADC at the local level. The lack of effort expended on behalf of women and children is indicated by the fact that only twenty-six states had approved ADC programs by 1936. Furthermore, Aid to Dependent Children meant just that: money went to the children and the parent or caretaker received nothing. The federal share of payment for one dependent child was one-third of $18 per month per family and one-third of $12 per month for any additional dependent children. This allotment was extremely low compared to other public assistance programs like Old Age Assistance to the needy elderly. The federal share of this program was one-half of $30 for each eligible elderly recipient (Abramovitz 1988). Once again this policy reflects the fundamental doctrine of the American welfare system that the worthy deserve more than the unworthy. Old people allegedly are not capable of competing in the labor market, so it is not their fault that they are poor.

The origins of the ADC program also demonstrate the historical schizophrenia surrounding ways in which political and social welfare leaders deal with policies that impact on the lives of women and small children. A woman's "natural" place is in the home where she is supported by her working husband. If that support ceases, she is usually thrown into financial crisis. Studies show that divorce, desertion, or the birth of a child significantly increase the probability that a woman will go on welfare (Hampton 1975; Dickenson 1975). If she applies for public assistance, she receives the lowest welfare benefits in the system; after all, she is able-bodied and should be out looking for a job. What moved the "natural" place of these women from the home into the labor market? One interpretation is that America has a double standard for women. Middle- and upper-class women belong at home, but lower-class women should be out working. Throughout history, poor women and women of color were expected to perform physically strenuous labor in the fields, while more affluent women were being told that factory and other manual labor jobs were "men's work."

Escalation of Female Poverty: 1940-1960

Expansion of the military industrial complex in the 1940s leading up to World War II and increases in the labor force brought relative prosperity to America. Women in increasing numbers went to work, while men marched off to war. In 1940, 24 percent of all women of working age were in the labor force. In 1943, the unemployment rate was as low as 1.2 percent. Throughout the Eisenhower presidency, unemployment averaged 4.5 percent; 5.7 percent between 1960 and

1965; and 3.8 percent between 1965 and 1970. These low percentages lulled politicians and social welfare policy planners into believing that a sense of prosperity existed for all Americans. Slowly the reality of inequality became evident for certain groups within the population. In 1960, the unemployment rate for whites was 4.9 percent in contrast to a rate of 10.2 percent for nonwhites. The unemployment rate among teenagers was 14.7 percent. Male- headed families were rapidly rising out of poverty, but it was due to the entrance of their wives into the labor force. On the other hand, by the end of the 1960s, these women's wages averaged only 59 percent of wages paid to male workers (Economic Report of the President: 1973).

In the 1950s, some expansion and liberalization occurred in public welfare programs including ADC. In 1950, a caretaker provision was added to ADC whereby the federal government provided some support for the parent of a dependent child. In 1956, federal funding for social services was added to ADC, and child welfare services were expanded in 1958 to include both rural and urban areas.

During the final years of the Eisenhower Administration, a migration of blacks to Northern urban areas from the rural South increased the pressure of rising unemployment on a sluggish economy. Many of those migrating were single women with dependent children. The migration demonstrated the existence of unequal access to education, employment, and housing, particularly among minorities in America. "The number of persons receiving public assistance more than doubled from 1960 to 1970, from approximately six to twelve million, as did the amount of money distributed to them, which increased from about $3.1 billion to well over $6 billion. Of the six million new recipients between 1960 and 1970, about five million were in various Aid to Families with Dependent Children (A.F.D.C.) programs" (Trattner 1979, pp. 249-250).

When the welfare rolls did go up in the 1960s, studies showed that the beneficiaries were predominantly residents who had lived in those cities and not the migrants from the South as believed. Piven and Cloward (1971) explain that "the relationship between widespread economic deprivation and the expansion of relief arrangements is neither direct nor simple" (p. 219). They contend that economic deprivation of large numbers of people is not enough to motivate the government to provide relief. When economic deprivation is accompanied by threats of civil disorder, then the government finds the means to expand welfare programs. One of the purposes that public welfare does serve is social control. The equitable redistribution of economic resources to reduce deprivation among the poor and disenfranchised is not a top priority of capitalism. History demonstrates that social welfare policy planners have become passive reinforcers of an ineffective and oppressive welfare state.

Similar to the activities of social workers during the Depression, social workers in the 1950s and 1960s acted in support of convention. Meyer (1970) observes that "Social work leadership continued to be closeted in bureaucratic cubbyholes, lobbying quietly on behalf of its version of progressive legislation and operating in a depersonalized role as an interpreter of issues" (p. 22).

In the 1960s, yet another noteworthy trend in public welfare began to unfold that demanded the attention of social welfare policy planners. By 1960, there were 3 million participants in the ADC program. Expenditures for ADC increased between 1950 and 1960 by 92 percent to total more than $1 billion. During 1961, the first year of John F. Kennedy's presidency, the number of ADC recipients increased another 502,000; expenditures for the year rose to $1.2 billion (U.S. Department of Health, Education, and Welfare, Social Security Administration 1961).

Rather than analyzing the structural factors that were causing the rise in female poverty, such as the lack of jobs for unskilled and undereducated female workers and the lack of day care services, federal and state officials initiated increasingly punitive and shortsighted measures in attempts to reduce the ADC rolls. State residency laws were strictly enforced which prevented blacks, who were moving from the South to Northern cities, from being eligible for assistance. Names of ADC recipients were published in local newspapers to cause embarrassment and deter potential applicants. Supposedly to check welfare fraud, entire caseloads were closed, and recipients had to endure the bureaucratic and lengthy application procedures all over again. Traditional, white, Anglo-Saxon, standards of sexual morality were used to judge whether recipients were worthy of receiving benefits. In some states, if an unrelated man was found living in the home, it was declared unfit for children. "In the summer of 1960 the state of Louisiana was found to have used the "suitable home" pretext for closing 6,281 cases, involving 23,549 children" (Axinn & Levin 1975, p. 236).

It was a commonly accepted procedure up until the late 1960s for public welfare caseworkers to conduct "midnight raids." These raids consisted of workers trying to catch ADC mothers in bed with husbands or boyfriends in order to have documented proof that there was a husband in the house. If it was a boyfriend rather than a husband, then that provided sufficient evidence to prove that the home was not a suitable one in which to raise children. Caseworkers would literally sneak around recipients' homes and peek into bedroom windows in the middle of the night to attempt to catch violators "in the act". In 1967, the Supreme Court of California declared that public assistance workers could not be fired for refusing to participate in an unconstitutional invasion of privacy (Parrish v. The Civil Service Commission of the County of Alameda, S.F. 1967). Man-in-the-house rules were declared unconstitutional in 1968 by the United States Supreme Court (King v. Smith 1968).

The escalating ADC rolls resulted in an increase in animosity towards recipients. Women on ADC were thought to be lazy and unmotivated; they were viewed as immoral women having babies in order to receive higher benefits. This was similar to the philosophy espoused by the proponents of The Elizabethan Poor Laws and the founders of the Charity Organization Society movement which viewed poor women as morally deficient. It was their own fault that they were poor. In reality, the main factor in explaining the rise in female poverty was not the increasing rate of poverty for women and children but rather a structural issue within the family. The rising proportion of poor women and children was, and currently is, due to the increase in households headed by women.

For white, female-headed households the poverty rate (the percentage of all people of a given type living below the poverty line) has not fluctuated significantly over the past twenty years. What has changed dramatically is the number of female-headed families. In 1965, there were 3.9 million white, female-headed households. By 1990, there were 7.3 million. Poor, white, female-headed households increased 52 percent from 1.2 million in 1959 to 2 million in 1990.

For black women, both the poverty rate and the number of black, female-headed households have risen. In 1959, there were 947,000 black, female-headed households; by 1990, there were 3.3 million. In the 1970s, the number of black, female-headed households doubled. Poor, black, female-headed households increased 180 percent from 551,000 in 1959 to 1.6 million in 1990.

For Spanish-origin households, the rise in female poverty is due to two factors: the increasing number of Spanish-origin families living in America and the rise in Spanish-origin, female-headed households. In 1974, there were 462,000 Hispanic-origin, female-headed households; by 1990, the number had risen to 1.1 million. Poor, Spanish- origin, female-headed households increased 128 percent from 211,000 in 1972 to 573.000 by 1990 (U.S. Bureau of the Census 1991).

In 1962, President Kennedy signed the Public Welfare Amendments to the Social Security Act in an attempt to stem the rising tide of ADC rolls and the increasing numbers of poor women and children. Because poverty among women was judged to be a problem within the individuals themselves rather than within the patriarchal family structure and the sexist job market, the Amendments sought solutions in employment training and work incentive programs and in individual counseling. If poor women could be rehabilitated through counseling and work training, they would then be able to get jobs and become financially independent of public assistance. The focus was on educating, counseling, and training the individual woman. If she failed to become financially independent, then she will be blamed rather than the government that provided her with a plethora of incentives and opportunities.

Nowhere is the issue of the sexual division of labor addressed or even acknowledged. Studies have shown that for middle-and upper-class women, education and training are not enough to break through the structural barriers of sexual inequality (Beck, Horan, & Tolbert 1978; England 1982; Duncan & Corcoran 1984). For poor women, it is practically impossible to overcome educational handicaps and sexual discrimination in the job market. Job opportunities are in the secondary labor market, and poor women simply cannot afford to support families on minimum wage jobs, pay health insurance premiums, and afford child care costs. The logical alternative is to stay on public assistance which provides some financial stability and medical coverage through Medicaid.

The main impact of the Public Welfare Amendments of 1962 on Title IV, Aid to Dependent Children, was to change the name of the program to Aid and Services to Needy Families with Children. The program would thus be called Aid to Families with Dependent Children or AFDC (U.S. Congress, House of Representatives 1962). As far as the impact on provision of services, the Amendments recommended the same individualistic solutions that social welfare policy analysts suggested back in the 1930s.

The War on Poverty and the Economic Opportunity Act

In 1964, President Lyndon B. Johnson declared a war on poverty and skillfully moved the Economic Opportunity Act through the legislative branches of the government. It signaled the beginning of the most massive federal government intervention in poverty programs in our nation's history. The welfare programs implemented under the Economic Opportunity Act were simply newer versions of older programs tried before. As in the past, social problems were viewed as temporary disruptions that could be resolved by funding reeducation and resocialization programs. The victims continued to be blamed for social problems and were the focus of intervention rather than the social, political, and economic systems. As Galper (1975) notes, "The War on Poverty and the categorical assistance programs focused their interventions on training, social services, casework treatment and so on. They did not establish and would not have had any mechanism to accomplish specific goals for the national redistribution of income" (p. 32).

By the time the war on poverty was declared, Aid to Families with Dependent Children rolls were rising dramatically. Public resentment against AFDC recipients was increasing, and politicians began jumping on the reform bandwagon. In December of 1964, a total of 1 million families received assistance; the total number of recipients had reached more than 4 million, including more than 3 million children. Title V of The Economic Opportunity Act, termed "Family Unity Through Jobs," funded short-term training and retraining courses leading to the transfer of trainees from relief rolls to jobs. Its central concern was for unemployed parents, both fathers and mothers, receiving assistance through the AFDC-UP program. Aid to Families with Dependent Children-- Unemployed Parent was instituted in 1961 as a variation of AFDC; fewer than one-half of the states chose to implement the program, and the eligibility requirements were so strict that few families with unemployed fathers were eligible for this program. It provides income to families in which both parents are present, but one or both are chronically unemployed. Presidential Assistant Sargent Shriver stated that Title V was meant to "demonstrate that public assistance with work and training can be used as a positive instrument to keep families together, to increase employability, and to brighten our communities" (Axinn & Levin 1975, p. 247).

Predictably the number of AFDC recipients continued to rise, and expenditures continued to increase throughout the 1960s. Rather than looking at the institutionalized sexist economic and political system that hinders women's rise out of poverty, new welfare policies were passed by Congress that punished AFDC recipients for being poor. The Social Security Amendments of 1967 were a perplexing combination of conflicting policies that resulted in no long-term welfare reform. The new law imposed a freeze on the number of children under twenty-one years of age who would be permitted to receive AFDC benefits because of absence of a parent from the household. Exempted from this eligibility freeze were children under twenty-one whose fathers (not mothers) had died or whose parents were unemployed. Those affected by the freeze were children whose fathers had deserted or who were "illegitimate." The moral overtone of this ruling echos back to the original ADC category in the Social Security Act of 1935 that covered widows but not divorced women. The premise is that families in which fathers desert or in which mothers have children outside of marriage deserve to be poor. It is their own irresponsible and immoral actions that caused their problems. State officials and social welfare professionals protested vociferously, and Congress repealed the freeze in 1969.

Another provision of the Social Security Amendments of 1967 was the establishment of a Work Incentive Program (WIN). Initially, the federal government referred to this program as WIP; understandably, it was a public relations nightmare, and the name was quickly changed to WIN. AFDC recipients, who are mostly women, had to accept employment or participate in job training programs if there were no children at home under six years of age. If they refused, they were denied benefits. In order to increase work incentives, recipients were allowed to keep the first $30 earned and one-third of subsequent earnings before facing reductions in their AFDC grants. Prior to this incentive, all reported income reduced recipients' grants or made them ineligible.

Liberals lobbied successfully against the conservatives to obtain a series of exceptions to the law that excused women receiving AFDC from the work requirement if they could prove that they were sick or if work was "inimical" to the health and welfare of the family. Due to these exemptions, relatively few women on AFDC were forced to seek employment. Liberals rejoiced at their victory because they viewed the mandatory work requirement as punitive and coercive. Their intentions were good, but their vision of welfare reform was narrow. Rather than myopically focusing on weakening the new work requirements of the

WIN program, liberals might have proposed public and private work opportunity programs that mandated that jobs in the segregated primary labor market be opened to women for equal pay. They might have developed comparable worth strategies. They might have proposed subsidized quality day-care programs, so poor women could afford to go to work. Instead of lobbying for long-term structural changes in the American economic system that would guarantee good jobs with equal pay and fair benefits for poor women, liberals were mollified by a short-term welfare reform compromise. Twenty years later in 1988, Senator Daniel P. Moynihan's Omnibus Welfare Reform Bill was approved by the U.S. Senate; it required all able-bodied welfare recipients, including AFDC parents with children over age three and, in some cases, age one, to enroll in state- designed job or training programs (JOBS). Four years later, the program is plagued by inadequate federal funding, and state compliance rates are low. Policy solutions that have proven ineffective in the past continue to be reintroduced as progressive change strategies.

In 1969, President Richard Nixon surprised liberals and conservatives alike when he proposed a national guaranteed annual income program as a solution to the rising AFDC rolls. He proposed the passage of a Family Assistance Plan (FAP) to replace AFDC and AFDC-UP that would establish a minimal standard of income at the federal level for all families and provide federal assistance to those who fell below that income level. It was not an income redistribution program by any means; in fact, increased costs to the federal government were projected to amount to only around $4.5 billion. It caused a furor, nevertheless, among liberal and conservative interest groups and was defeated in 1972.

A significant policy reform that was approved at that time was the federalization of all the other public assistance programs including Old Age Assistance, Aid to the Blind, and Aid to the Disabled. They came under the federal program called Supplemental Security Income or SSI. SSI is administered by the Social Security Administration, so recipients receive their monthly checks in the mail from the federal government. Because the program is federal, monthly benefits are higher than those received by women and children on AFDC which comes under the jurisdiction of individual states. If SSI recipients have problems, they no longer go to their local county welfare offices but to the local Social Security offices. The stigma of welfare has so effectively been removed from the SSI program that many of the elderly and disabled receiving SSI benefits do not perceive themselves as welfare recipients.

Why was Congress willing to federalize public assistance programs to the elderly and disabled and not to mothers with young children? What causes social welfare policy planners to recommend higher monthly benefits for the aged and disabled poor than for women and children who are poor? Senior citizen lobby groups have gained power and prestige over the past twenty years and do have an impact on Congressional legislation. It creates a poor image for legislators to be against the needs of the elderly or the handicapped; their life circumstances are not their fault, and they cannot be expected to work. On the other hand, able-bodied women with children and no husbands are easy targets of anti-welfare and misogynistic sentiments. They are accused of laziness, immoral sexual conduct, and unwillingness to find jobs. They are undeserving of benefits because if they really wanted to get off AFDC, they could. They simply are not trying hard enough.

The Legacy of Reaganomics

The 1980 election of Ronald Reagan during a rise in conservatism in America had devastating effects on poor women and children. He swept into office promising to cut the federal budget and lower the huge deficit. Although the entitlement programs such as Social Security and Medicare constituted over half of federal spending on social programs, he continued current levels of funding due to their powerful and vocal constituencies. Entitlements constituted 41 percent of the nation's spending in 1980; indeed, Social Security alone constituted almost 33 percent of the nation's domestic budget. Reagan was therefore forced to take all of the $50 billion in proposed cuts from those programs that specifically gave services and resources to poor persons (Meyer 1984).

The rising inflation rate of the 1970s and no increases in AFDC benefits during that period combined to actually erode the real value of AFDC benefits. Add Reagan's proposed cuts to that erosion of benefits and the results were increasingly oppressive for poor women. At the same time Reagan was proposing further reductions in the already below poverty level benefits for poor women and children, he was supporting dramatic increases in defense spending that support the military industrial complex.

In 1981, Reagan's budget cuts were approved through the passage of the Omnibus Budget Reconciliation Act (OBRA).

Means-tested programs, in particular AFDC, shouldered the brunt of the reductions. The work incentive program, which permitted AFDC recipients to keep part of their earnings without affecting their grants, was repealed by Congress. After four months, every dollar earned would be subtracted from AFDC benefits. Reagan's welfare reduction plan has been particularly unfair to the working poor of whom most are women trying to support families by themselves. He considers it a waste of money to help low- income, working families. Meyer (1984) observes that "the wide array of special tax breaks and other subsidies flowing permanently to middle- and upper-income households remains unchecked. This unique treatment of the working poor is a major source of unfairness in administration policy" (p. 56).

It is ironic that a president who vigorously campaigned on a platform that strongly supported the American work ethic proposed welfare reforms that provided disincentives to work for AFDC mothers. Reagan's budget cuts forced many working women in minimum-wage jobs to return to the welfare rolls.

The AFDC cutbacks were sexist actions that reinforced the powerlessness of low income and poor women. In 1987, the average AFDC cash grant for a single-parent family with two children was $354 per month (O'Hare 1987). This is one-half the monthly income necessary to meet the national poverty level established by the federal government. The federal government establishes a national poverty level which sets the minimum level of subsistence that a family can live on in America. In every state, AFDC monthly grants fall below the established poverty level.

The Reagan Revolution failed. Due to tax cuts and the creation of tax loopholes for businesses, large increases in the military budget, and soaring costs of Social Security and Medicare, the United States currently has an unprecedented and skyrocketing federal deficit. A majority of the beneficiaries of tax cuts, military spending, and social insurance expenditures are middle- and upper-income, white males. At the same time, the Reagan Administration implemented drastic cuts in welfare spending for programs that served the neediest segments of the population. Poor women and children have no powerful lobbies in Washington to fight for their cause, and few politicians want to go on record in support of unemployed, single women having babies. Although AFDC was already one of the lowest budgeted programs in the welfare system, its budget was cut. This is the legacy of Reaganomics.

Reagan's conservative agenda gained support with the election of his Vice President, George Bush, in 1988. Poor women and children continue to struggle to survive in America in the 1990s. The largest population group being assisted in emergency shelters for the homeless is women and their young children. One in four children under the age of six lives in poverty. During the Reagan and Bush presidencies, the percentage of all Americans living in poverty has risen to 13.5 percent. The following chapter provides a statistical overview of the feminization of poverty and documents the impact of sexist social welfare policies on women and children of America.

POVERTY AS A MEANS OF DOMINATION

Statistical Overview of the Feminization of Poverty

Institutionalized discrimination against women is a subtle yet pervasive problem. Some progress has been made since the early 1900s when women were viewed as property and treated as slaves by their fathers and husbands; however, economic parity and legal and social equality remain major problems today. "For men, poverty is often the consequence of unemployment and a job is generally an effective remedy. While female poverty often exists even when a woman works full-time" (Burnham 1986, p. 74). Many poor women of working age are already working, but their wages are so low and their benefits so inadequate that they cannot support their children. In 1983, for example, men were two and a half times more likely than women to work full time for over 50 weeks (53.6 percent for men versus 21.3 percent for women). Using data across all levels of the occupational hierarchy, the average woman's wages were 47 percent below the average man's wages. The average income of female workers was below the federally established poverty threshold for a family of four (U.S. Bureau of the Census 1983). Because of jobs that pay below poverty-level wages, many working women with families to support end up applying for public welfare.

One of the outcomes of discrimination against women is the phenomenon termed the "feminization of poverty." It refers to the growing percentage of all poor Americans who are women and their dependents. The rate of female poverty has been so dramatic and steady over the past twenty-five years that women and their children now constitute the largest group of poor people in America. The large rise in the percentage of all households headed by women is the crucial reason for the feminization of poverty. There is a strong correlation between women heading households and poverty because female-headed households have extremely high rates of poverty.

Some feminist scholars are critical of the concept of the "feminization of poverty." They argue that it wrongly shifts the focus of the analysis of women's oppression from class exploitation and racism to gender (Burnham 1986; Higginbotham 1986). I disagree with this critique because Marxism's analysis of class oppression and liberalism's analysis of racial inequality have been gender-blind. Both theoretical perspectives have lacked an understanding of patriarchy and of how males have used power and domination to oppress women.

Class and race must necessarily be included in an analysis of poverty and women but within the context of gender.

Before providing a statistical overview of female poverty, the general concept of poverty itself needs to be defined. Families and unrelated individuals are classified as being above or below the poverty level using the poverty index originated at the Social Security Administration in 1964. The poverty index is based on the Department of Agriculture's 1961 Economy Food Plan and reflects the different consumption requirements of families based on their size and composition. It was determined from the Department of Agriculture's 1955 Survey of Food Consumption that families of three or more persons spend approximately one-third of their income on food; the poverty level for these families was, therefore, set at three times the cost of the Economy Food Plan. The poverty index is based solely on money income and does not reflect noncash benefits such as food stamps, Medicaid, and public housing. The poverty thresholds are updated every year to reflect changes in the Consumer Price Index (CPI). The average poverty threshold for a family of four was $13,359 in 1990, $12,674 in 1989, $12,091 in 1988, $11,611 in 1987, and $11,203 in 1986 (U.S. Bureau of the Census 1991). It bears repeating that every state pays AFDC recipients less than the poverty threshold.

A review of the poverty status of the general population provides a baseline data with which to compare female poverty statistics. Because the Economic Opportunity Act legislated unprecedented amounts of federal funding at the local level to wage a "war on poverty," the poverty rate dropped dramatically during the 1960s. The percent of persons below the poverty level dropped from 22.1 to 11.1 percent between 1960 and 1973; during the decade, the number of persons below the poverty level was reduced from 39.9 to 23 million. Throughout the 1970s, there were minor fluctuations in poverty trends. From 1978 to 1983, however, the Reagan Revolution evolved, and the number of persons in poverty increased by 44 percent, from 24.5 to 35.3 million, and the poverty rate rose from 11 to 15 percent. In 1990, the number of persons in poverty was 33.5 million, and the poverty rate was 13.5 percent (U.S. Bureau of the Census 1991).

Statistics on families in poverty reflect the rising trend in female poverty among single heads of households. The number of poor families in 1990 was 7.1 million. Since 1983, the number of poor families has decreased from 7.6 to 7.1 million, and their poverty rate has dropped slightly from 12.3 to 10.7 percent. Similarly, the number of married-couple families below the poverty level has decreased from 3.8 million to 3 million, and their poverty rate has been lowered from 7.6 to 5.7 percent. On the other hand, the number of poor families headed by females has averaged 3.6 million, and their poverty rate has remained around 35 percent since 1983 (U.S. Bureau of the Census 1991). The disproportionate number and rate of poverty among women heading households compared to all poor families and married-couple families are illustrated on Table 1 and Table 2.

Table 1

Percent of Families Below the Poverty Level:
1990, 1985, and 1983

Characteristic	1990	1985	1983
All Families	10.7	11.4	12.3
White	8.1	9.1	9.7
Black	29.3	28.7	32.3
Hispanic*	25.0	25.5	25.9
Married-couple Families	5.7	6.7	7.6
Male householder, no wife present	12.0	12.9	13.2
Female householder, no husband present	33.4	34.0	36.0

*Persons of Hispanic origin may be of any race.

Source: U.S. Bureau of the Census. (1991). Poverty in the United States: 1990. <u>Current Population Reports</u>. (Series P-60, No. 175).

Table 2

Number of Families Below the Poverty Line:
1990, 1985, and 1983

(Numbers in thousands)

Characteristic	1990	1985	1983
All Families	7,098	7,223	7,647
White	4,622	4,983	5,220
Black	2,193	1,983	2,161
Hispanic*	1,244	1,074	981
Married-Couple Families	2,981	3,438	3,815
Male householder, no wife present	349	311	268
Female householder, no husband present	3,768	3,474	3,564

*Persons of Hispanic origin may be of any race.

Source: U.S. Bureau of the Census. (1991). Poverty in the United States: 1990. <u>Current Population Reports</u>. (Series P-60, No. 175).

Statistics demonstrate that the feminization of poverty is mostly the result of increasing poverty among single women and their dependent children (Pearce 1986; Rodgers 1986; Sidel 1986; Kamerman & Kahn 1988). The structural barriers in the system that result in two out of every three poor adults being women include antiquated divorce and separation laws, unequal access to employment opportunities, low wages, below poverty level welfare benefits, and inadequate or nonexistent support for care of children. A review of demographic data on poverty and gender illustrates the serious nature of the problem of the feminization of poverty.

Between 1959 and 1990, the number of families maintained by women with no husband present increased from 9.8 percent to 17 percent of all families and from 6.8 to 12.7 percent of all nonpoor families. In 1959 only 23 percent of all poor families were headed by a women; by 1990, the percentage had increased to 53.1 percent. In 1959 the number of poor female family heads was 1.9 million; by 1990, the figure had jumped to 3.3 million. Since 1959, the poverty rate for families with female householder has consistently been three times higher than the poverty rate for all poor families. In 1990 the poverty rate for poor families was 10.7 percent; whereas, the poverty rate for female-headed households was 33.4 percent (see Table 3). This trend reflects a significant socioeconomic change in late twentieth century American capitalism.

The issue of the feminization of poverty has racial and ethnic implications. Since 1970, the rate of black families headed by single women has increased by approximately 75 percent; 60 percent of black families with children are now headed by single mothers. Although black female-headed families comprise half of the AFDC cases on a national level, they are concentrated in states that provide the lowest benefits (Folbre 1987; Kamerman & Kahn 1988). Hispanic women headed about 50 percent of poor Hispanic families in both 1973 (accurate census figures for Spanish-origin citizens have only been available since 1973) and in 1984 (Rodgers 1986).

Table 3

Number of Female Householder Families Below the Poverty Level and Poverty Rate: 1990 and 1959

(Numbers in thousands)

Characteristic	1990	1959
Number of poor families	7,098	8,320
Poverty rate for poor families	10.7	18.5
Number of poor families with female as householder	3,768	1,916
Poverty rate for families with female householder	33.4	42.6
Families with female householder as a percent of all poor families	53.1	23.0
Families with female householder as a percent of all non-poor families	12.7	6.8
Families with female householder as a percent of all families	17.0	9.8

Source: U.S. Bureau of the Census. (1991). Poverty in the United States: 1990. Current Population Reports. (Series P-60, No. 175).

Because increasing numbers of single mothers heading households are poor, it follows that poverty among children is a growing problem. There are more poor children now than in any year since 1965. About 13.4 million or 20.6% of children under the age of 18 live in poverty. The majority of these children are white; in 1990, 61% of all poor children were white or approximately 8.2 million children. The poverty rate for white children was 15.9%. This is the highest rate of poverty for white children since the early 1960s. In 1990, 34% of all poor children were black. There were 4.6 million poor black children, and the poverty rate for black children was 44.8%. The rate of poverty for black children is almost three times the rate for white children. Statistics for children of Spanish origin have only been available since 1973; however, poverty among Spanish-origin children is rising. In 1990, 21% of all poor children were of Spanish-origin. Poor Spanish-origin children numbered 2.9 million, and their poverty rate was 38.4% (see Table 4).

The growing number of poor children attests to the importance of political influence. Social welfare policy analysts and sociologists are predicting serious ramifications if steps are not taken to address the dual problem of female poverty and poverty among children, but politicians and other leaders have paid little attention to these trends. Children do not have power and influence, and they do not vote. The economic progress made by the elderly over the past twenty-five years exemplifies the power of political pressure.

In 1959, 35.2 percent of people over sixty-five were poor; in 1980, 15.7 percent. Between 1970 and 1983, the income of older Americans went up faster than that of those under sixty-five. One of the reasons for this change is that social security coverage was extended from 60 percent of the aging in 1960 to 92 percent in 1981 (Harrington 1984). In 1990, only 10.9 percent of the nation's poor were elderly; whereas, 40 percent of the poor were children (U.S. Bureau of the Census 1991). The elderly mobilized political and economic strategies that pressured politicians and business leaders into supporting their causes. The elderly are an established and powerful political lobby in Washington. The two main social welfare programs that are targeted for the elderly, Social Security and Medicare, are the most costly and most rapidly expanding programs in the national welfare system. None of Bush's most conservative advisors nor any politicians from either major party dare to propose reductions in the programs budgeted for the elderly for fear of swift and vocal political repercussions.

Table 4

Number of Children Below the Poverty Level by Race of
Family Head: 1990, 1973, and 1965

(Numbers in thousands)

Characteristic	1990	1973	1965
All related children under 18	13,431	9,453	14,388
Poverty rate	20.6	14.2	20.7
White family head	8,232	5,462	8,595
Percent of all poor children	61.3	57.8	59.7
Poverty rate	15.9	9.7	14.4
Black family head	4,550	3,822	5,022
Percent of all poor children	33.9	40.4	35.0
Poverty rate	44.8	40.6	65.5
Spanish-origin family head	2,865	1,364	*
Percent of all poor children	21.3	14.4	*
Poverty rate	38.4	27.8	*

*Statistics not available until 1973.

Source: U.S. Bureau of the Census. (1991). Poverty in the United States: 1990. Current Population Reports. (Series P-60, No. 175).

In conclusion, the data indicate that the fastest growing type of family in America is that headed by a single woman. The number of female-headed families has increased dramatically due to the rising rates of divorce, separation, and single parenting. Female-headed families tend to be poor due to factors related to underemployment, unemployment, and Aid to Families with Dependent Children benefits that are far below federally established poverty threshold levels.

Some of the current liberal policy reforms under discussion to aid families headed by women include broadening child-care options that are both publicly and privately supported, enforcing child support laws, instituting maternity leaves, improving educational opportunities for all children of school age, and expanding tax reforms to help low-income families. Sex education is yet another liberal reform policy proposed to reduce the size and number of female-headed households. Of particular concern are the rising number of households being set up by teenagers who become pregnant. As the historical review of social welfare policy emphasizes, movements for policy reform usually focus on the individual because individuals are deemed at fault or personally deficient for having social problems that they cannot solve themselves.

In the final chapter, I propose a progressive feminist social welfare agenda that will not merely reduce poverty among women and children but prevent and eliminate it. Before discussing that agenda, the repressive nature of the current American federal welfare system and its inequitable expenditures need to be understood and analyzed from a socialist feminist perspective.

THE POLITICAL STRUCTURE'S RESPONSE: THE AMERICAN SOCIAL WELFARE SYSTEM

Social Welfare Policy Issues

As the historical review of American social welfare policy and poverty trends has demonstrated, American capitalism, from its inception, established a system for dealing with women that was paternalistic, oppressive and moralistic. The married man is the producer or breadwinner and always in charge of the woman and children; therefore, capitalism directs the majority of economic incentives and advantages toward him. On the other hand, capitalism assigns the married woman to the role of a nonproductive housewife who performs wifely duties and domestic chores with no financial rewards. When this traditional system breaks down, social welfare policies and marriage laws benefit men more than women. After divorce, separation, or death of a spouse, the man's economic situation improves; the woman's plight usually deteriorates.

If a woman has never been legally married, then she has consistently experienced the economic and legal sanctions against single women in our society. Inequitable tax laws favor married couples and couples with children. Unmarried women pay the same Social Security taxes as married workers, yet they are entitled to differential benefits. In addition, welfare benefits for single mothers are lower than those for the disabled, elderly, or blind.

The roots of sexist policy making in America can be traced back to the Depression of the 1930s. It resulted in a major transformation in the way in which society viewed unemployment and poverty in America. Social unrest among the working class led to massive federal intervention in relief programs to help the poor (Piven & Cloward 1971). Labor union lobbying efforts resulted in the establishment of New Deal welfare policies that mainly focused on returning white males to gainful employment.

Political turmoil is not usually emphasized as a contributing factor to the passage of the Social Security Act of 1935. The interpretation preferred is one that shows political and corporate leaders altruistically and willingly responding to the needs of the people. In actuality, the paternalistic leadership in America waited as long as possible and responded slowly and cautiously to civil uprising only when it was no longer economically or politically feasible to prevent mass insurrection. When the government's response finally did come, it was designed to ease the economic needs of white males.

The Social Security Act instituted dramatic changes in the principles and practices of the American social welfare institution, but most of the new policies simply reinforced existing sexist ideology. It ushered in a new era of federal responsibility for social welfare programs, but what that responsibility entailed was not clearly defined. "Therefore, the American welfare state developed without a self-conscious sense of political struggle, leaving the apolitical planners and administrators as well as the workers, within the public and private system, with a confusion regarding their basic goals and direction" (Withorn 1985, p. 23). The Roosevelt Administration's initial lack of vision resulted in fifty years of social welfare programs biased against women, minorities, and the poor.

Since the time of the Depression, the provisions of the national social welfare system have broadened and increased significantly to encompass expanding numbers of middle- and upper-income recipients. Concurrently, provisions to the poor have been repeatedly reduced under the Reagan and Bush administrations which have relied heavily upon the conviction that social welfare efforts should be the responsibility of the private sector and the states. Under President Reagan's and Bush's social welfare policies, many poor people are not eligible for welfare benefits, while increasing numbers of middle- and upper-class individuals are reaping larger and expanding benefits from social programs. The Changing Domestic Priorities Project of The Urban Institute sponsored a conference to address the aims and outcomes of the Reagan administration's social welfare policy. One of the main conclusions was that "The budget reductions for social welfare were not equally distributed across programs: the deepest cuts were made in means-tested programs targeted on the nonaged poor, while the social insurance programs--Social Security, Medicare, and veterans' benefits--were affected much less;..." (Gorham 1984, p. 3).

The largest proportion of government spending on social programs supports "non-means-tested" programs such as Social Security, Unemployment Insurance, and Medicare rather than "means-tested" programs which provide direct grants or services to poor people. In 1988 federal expenditures for Social Security Retirement, Survivors, and Disability totaled $216.4 billion while $65.9 billion of federal funds were spent for AFDC, Medicaid, SSI [Supplemental Security Income], and Food Stamps combined. In 1985 only 11 percent of the $950 billion federal budget went to support means-tested programs (O'Hare 1987).

A great deal of confusion and misinformation surround the present-day social welfare system. A broad dichotomy exists between what the public perceives public welfare to be and what it actually is. Before discussing welfare programs and expenditures, several basic social welfare policy issues need to be analyzed; they reflect the philosophical and ethical foundation upon which the American welfare system is based.

Welfare policy issues stimulate ongoing philosophical debates between conservatives and liberals about the proper role the state should play in providing social welfare services. When the arguments quiet and the rhetoric slows down, the most consistent and fundamental philosophical concern of politicians and social welfare policy planners has been to preserve the traditional "family ethic." Social welfare policies and practices have favored men and women who have followed the traditional roles of male breadwinner and female homemaker. Poor women and women of color are chastised by the system for following atypical lifestyles (Abramovitz 1988). Abramovitz's family ethic critique provides a unique way of viewing social welfare policy through a gender lens.

The repressive nature of social welfare policy becomes increasingly evident when analyzed from the perspective of gender and marital status. Poor women and women of color are treated particularly harshly. Throughout history, the role of women has been that of reproduction; their place has been in the home passively rearing children and performing household tasks. Men's role has been that of production; their place has been out in the capitalist labor market aggressively competing for power and money. Under the rules and regulations dictated by social welfare policy, divergence from these paternalistic norms results in unequal treatment for women.

For example, the first mothers' pension legislation covered widows with children but not other single mothers who were divorced, separated or unmarried. The latter group of women were deemed immoral and unworthy of assistance. Social welfare policy planners have repeatedly forced poor women and women of color to seek jobs in the unskilled and low paying secondary labor market, while they simultaneously supported the ethic of staying at home for middle- and upper-class women.

The largest program in the social welfare system, Social Security, provides benefits only to those who have a consistent work history and to their spouses and children. This policy penalizes many women who are homemakers and/or women who have transitory or part-time labor force participation. Not until 1950 were working women's surviving children even covered under Social Security; it took until 1975 for a Supreme Court ruling to extend Social Security coverage to surviving husbands of female workers. Those marginally employed or those lacking the skills and education to enter the competitive labor market, such as many single heads of households and welfare mothers, are ineligible to receive benefits.

When women do meet the eligibility requirements for Social Security, preferential treatment is afforded to those who have been traditional heterosexual wives who stayed home, reproduced children, and did housework. Their benefits are based on the husbands' work history. The formula for monthly Social Security benefits is based on number of years worked and salary earned. Because men have more permanent labor force attachment and receive higher wages, married women often receive better Social Security benefits than single women, women who have stayed home as housewifes are rewarded more than those wives who have worked, and families in which there has been one wage earner often receive more benefits than those in which there have been two wage earners (Abramovitz 1986).

A second major social welfare policy issue is whether the institution of social welfare should provide either institutional services or residual services. Institutional services are considered rights and available to all people. They are "the organized system of social services and institutions, designed to aid individuals and groups to attain satisfying standards of life and health. It aims at personal and social relationships which permit individuals the fullest development of their capacities and the promotion of their well-being in harmony with the needs of the community" (Wilensky & Lebeaux 1965, p. 139). This liberal view of social welfare services implies no stigma and no abnormality; social welfare becomes accepted as a proper and legitimate function of modern industrial society. On the other hand, residual services require that strict and restrictive eligibility standards be established and only distributed when the normal structures of the family and the economic market break down. This conservative view of welfare services stigmatizes welfare as charity and a public shame.

The American conception of social welfare is more supportive of the residual model, yet the dramatic expansion of certain entitlement programs to the general population supports the institutional model. The American philosophy of rugged individualism is strongly reflected in its punitive social welfare policies that affect programs that benefit the poor and disenfranchised. Tedious bureaucratic procedures discourage many potential public assistance recipients; if they do apply and meet eligibility criteria, they are subjected to public condemnation of their inability to achieve financial success. On the other hand, federal spending on social programs that affect the middle and upper classes, such as Social Security and Medicare, has increased.

Rather than debating the strengths and weaknesses of the residual model versus the institutional model, I argue for a radically different model of social welfare services that requires conceptual rethinking and systemic restructuring rather than recycled reforms. I propose a socialist feminist model of social welfare services in which equality would replace inegalitarianism, in which cooperation would replace competition, in which self- determination and integrity would replace exploitation and oppression, and in which justice would prevail over sexual, racial, and class injustice. This progressive feminist social welfare agenda is discussed in the final chapter.

The final social welfare policy issue concerns the funding of social welfare expenditures. Historically, conservatives support local responsibility for funding welfare programs at the state and county levels and encourage private funding to supplement any deficits. Liberals tend to promote the expansion of the federal government's involvement in welfare programs in order to encourage the national standardization of benefits and promote equality of services. Welfare services under state and local auspices vary greatly; eligibility requirements are more restrictive, and standards are generally lower. The argument offered by most state and county officials for inequities in cash assistance programs across the country is that benefits reflect the different cost of living standards in each state.

Federal involvement in welfare services requires uniform programs throughout the nation and national regulations for eligibility with fewer restrictions. This usually results in higher standards for the delivery of services. One of the concerns with the federalization of welfare services is the cost factor. Many politicians relish running on platforms that recommend cutbacks in welfare costs. What most politicians fail to publicly clarify is that rising federal spending for human resource programs is highly correlated with the escalating costs of Social Security and Medicare.

The 1990 Budget Perspectives, which reviews federal expenditures for social welfare programs, examines constant dollar spending trends for human resource programs over the past twenty years. Current dollars represent the amount actually spent in a given year; constant dollars represent the amount spent in a given year, adjusted for inflation. Spending for years before 1985 have been inflated to 1985 dollars in order to account for the declining value of dollars spent over the 1966 to 1990 period. The Report's findings demonstrate the importance of objectively analyzing social welfare expenditures lest one uncritically accept the sexist and racist ideology that is perpetuated about welfare recipients.

Whereas total human resource spending increased by 248 percent or $336 billion over the past twenty years, that increase is due in large part to Social Security legislation that established automatic cost-of-living adjustments (COLAs). Social Security accounted for 37 percent of that increase, and Medicare accounted for 20 percent. Since 1975 the elderly and disabled workers have received repeated raises in Social Security benefits. Social Security spending has increased 197 percent between 1966 and 1985 from $63 billion to $189 billion. The increase in human resource spending is also due to rising Medicare costs. Medicare costs have escalated from $196 million in 1966 to $66 billion in 1985 (U.S. Library of Congress 1986). Table 5 outlines federal outlays for all the human resource programs in 1985 constant dollars since 1966 to 1992. In 1992, $277 billion is budgeted for Social Security and $121 billion for Medicare.

The two largest and most costly social welfare programs are the ones that assist individuals with consistent work histories. When Reagan's welfare cutbacks were enacted in the early 1980s, these two programs lost no federal funds. Federal expenditures for AFDC, the welfare program targeted for poor single mothers with dependent children, were significantly reduced.

The preceding discussion has focused on the main policy issues that shape and guide welfare programs and services. It is time to look at specific social welfare programs and their costs.

Table 5

Federal Outlays for Human Resource Programs: 1966-1992

(Numbers in millions of constant 1985 dollars)

Fiscal Year	Education, Training, Employment & Social Services	Health	Medicare	Income Security
1966	$16,532	$ 7,798	$ 196	$ 29,628
1967	23,013	9,981	8,230	31,542
1968	25,644	12,665	13,369	34,909
1969	23,960	14,244	15,715	34,274
1970	25,557	15,590	16,397	41,290
1971	27,375	17,272	16,714	57,890
1972	33,142	20,950	18,064	66,753
1973	31,605	21,655	18,637	65,418
1974	28,618	22,878	20,546	71,831
1975	33,554	25,108	25,001	97,402
1976	36,378	28,573	28,755	110,386
1977	37,400	29,203	32,651	103,032
1978	44,340	29,220	35,915	96,993
1979	46,391	29,762	38,476	96,367
1980	44,063	30,402	42,108	113,557
1981	42,390	32,071	46,734	119,043
1982	31,512	30,777	52,220	120,794
1983	29,322	30,809	56,568	131,877
1984	28,940	31,458	59,509	116,523
1985	29,343	33,542	65,822	128,200
1986	30,585	35,936	70,164	119,796
1987	29,724	39,968	75,120	123,250
1988	31,938	44,490	78,878	129,332
1989	36,351	49,761	86,734	136,947
1990 (est.)	39,531	52,177	94,918	136,788
1991 (est.)	39,934	56,743	107,077	142,468
1992 (est.)	38,987	61,484	120,877	148,624

Table 5 (Continued)

Federal Outlays for Human Resource Programs: 1966-1992

Fiscal Year	Social Security	Veterans' Benefits & Services	Total Human Resources
1966	$ 63,453	$ 18,163	$ 135,774
1967	65,268	20,555	158,588
1968	68,276	19,860	174,724
1969	75,325	21,087	184,604
1970	79,889	22,906	201,629
1971	90,540	24,679	234,470
1972	96,989	25,920	261,818
1973	113,621	27,809	278,746
1974	119,082	28,537	291,491
1975	125,554	32,232	338,850
1976	134,203	33,475	371,770
1977	143,569	30,445	376,301
1978	148,060	29,937	384,466
1979	151,136	28,944	391,077
1980	155,557	27,799	413,486
1981	166,627	27,445	434,310
1982	174,898	26,867	437,068
1983	183,645	26,726	458,947
1984	184,321	26,490	447,241
1985	188,623	26,352	471,882
1986	198,756	26,356	481,594
1987	207,352	26,782	502,197
1988	219,341	29,428	533,407
1989	232,334	29,218	571,344
1990 (est.)	246,724	29,872	600,011
1991 (est.)	262,254	30,574	639,049
1992 (est.)	276,793	31,350	678,115

Source: U.S. Office of Management and Budget. Congressional Research Service. (1989). Historical tables: Budget of the United States Government, fiscal year 1990.

Social Welfare Programs and Trends in Expenditures

One of the most persistent myths about American social welfare programs is that most of their resources go to the poor. Many of the poor do not receive welfare benefits, and many people who do receive welfare are not poor. Of the more than 33 million Americans living in poverty, less than half get assistance from the federal cash welfare programs (Schiller 1984). "Only seven of the 59 'major' welfare programs use the poverty level to determine eligibility" (O'Hare 1987). The welfare rolls have not expanded over the past ten years to keep pace with the growing poverty population.

The American version of a welfare state is confusing and complicated. Reports issued by the federal government offer inconsistent explanations about what programs are included in the welfare system. Generally speaking, there are three major categories of federal government assistance programs: (l) Social insurance transfers or entitlements; (2) Means-tested income transfers which include both (a) cash assistance or public assistance transfers and (b) in kind or noncash transfers; and (3) Education, training, and employment programs.

The social insurance transfer programs are non-means-tested and are based on employee and/or employer contributions; benefits are generally wage and work related. The programs in this category include: Social Security Retirement, Social Security Disability Insurance, Unemployment Insurance, Veterans' benefits and Medicare. (See Appendix for descriptions of individual programs.)

The means-tested income transfer programs benefit only those who meet low income requirements and other qualifications. Aid to Families with Dependent Children (AFDC) and Supplemental Security Income (SSI) are the two means-tested cash assistance programs to the poor. The means-tested noncash programs are Medicaid, Food Stamps, Public Housing, and School Lunch Programs. (See Appendix for descriptions of individual programs.)

Education, training, and employment programs were initially funded during the War On Poverty, and the goals of these programs are to teach the poor marketable job skills in order to integrate them successfully into the labor market. Funding for these program has always been minimal.

Table 6 outlines 1988 federal outlays for the major human resource programs; the Table also shows the percent of total federal

Table 6

Federal Expenditures for Major Human Resource Programs
Fiscal Year 1988
(Numbers in billions of dollars)

Program	Federal Outlays	Percent*
SOCIAL INSURANCE TRANSFERS		
Social Security Retirement, Survivors, & Disability	$216.4	41.4%
Medicare	83.6	16.0
Veterans' Benefits	28.9	5.5
Unemployment Insurance	15.3	2.9
Total	$344.2	65.8%
MEANS-TESTED INCOME TRANSFERS		
Cash Assistance Transfers		
Supplemental Security Income	$11.7	2.2%
Aid to Families with Dependent Children	10.3	2.0
Total	$22.0	4.2%
Noncash Transfers		
Medicaid	$30.6	5.9%
Food Stamps	13.3	2.5
Public & Subsidized Housing	11.6	2.2
School Lunch Programs	3.1	.6
Total	$58.6	11.2%
EDUCATION, TRAINING, & EMPLOYMENT		
Compensatory Education Aid	$10.0	1.9%
Social Services Block Grant	.4	.1
Employment & Job Training	3.8	.7
Total	$14.2	2.7%
Total for Major Programs Listed	$439.0	83.9%
Total Federal Expenditures on Human Resource Programs	$523.2	

*Percent of Total Federal Expenditures on Human Resource Programs
Sources: U.S. Library of Congress. Congressional Research Service. (October 1989). Cash and noncash benefits for persons with limited income: Eligibility rules, recipient and expenditure date, FY 1986-88. (No. 89-595); and U.S. Department of Health and Human Services. Social Security Administration. (May 1991). Social Security Bulletin.

expenditures spent on each major human resource program. The 16 percent of federal expenditures not listed on Table 6 includes small grants to state and local governments to help fund a variety of educational, vocational, and social service programs.

The vast majority of federal welfare spending supports those who are covered by work-related programs. Federal spending on these programs increased from 3.3 percent of GNP in 1966 to 7.1 percent in 1984 (Danziger & Weinberg 1986). Social Security Retirement and Disability, Unemployment Insurance, Veterans' benefits and Medicare represent 65.8 percent of federal welfare expenditures or $344.2 billion. Veterans benefits alone cost $28.9 billion which is almost three times the $10.3 billion budgeted by the federal government for the welfare program for poor women and their children, AFDC.

AFDC is criticized for being the largest means-tested cash assistance program. This is a true but deceptive claim because AFDC accounts for only 2 percent of the total $523 billion spent by the federal government on assistance programs. In fact, both means-tested cash assistance programs that are targeted for the poor, AFDC and SSI, account for only $22 billion or 4.2 percent of the total federal outlays for human resource programs; whereas, the social insurances account for 66 percent of total federal expenditures on human resource programs. "Interest on the national debt alone costs 13 times the federal expenditure on AFDC in fiscal year 1984--$111.0 billion versus $8.3 billion" (O'Hare 1985, p. 29).

A nation that expends 66 percent of its federal welfare budget in support of social insurance programs that assist more affluent citizens, while it spends a mere 2 percent to help poor, single mothers with small children is one that fosters gender, race, and class oppression. A nation that spends $295 billion on national defense in 1992 and only $10 billion on impoverished mothers and young children is one that gives military weapons priority over human welfare. The current economic policies of the Bush administration insure that consulting companies and defense contractors make profits in the millions, while welfare mothers struggle to feed, house, and clothe their children on three hundred dollars a month.

A conclusion that can be drawn from analyzing welfare expenditures is that the American welfare state exists to serve the needs of special interests groups that have lucratively funded political lobbies in Washington. "We are being taught about those interests by the Reagan administration's own proclamations that increased business profits are its goal and by its frank courting of America's business elite" (Piven & Cloward 1982, p. 143). The distribution of funds has shifted to favor the more secure in the population. The trend in government spending favors public employees, the retired, and those injured on the job. At the bottom of the current priority list for government funding are low-income, public assistance recipients who are blind, disabled, elderly, and single women with dependent children.

One of the reasons why poverty rates for women and children are increasing is because AFDC benefits have been declining over the past eight years and have not been adjusted to reflect inflation (Burtless 1986). On the other hand, Social Security and Supplemental Security Income (SSI) are linked to the Consumer Price Index and updated annually. These programs assist the more privileged members of society who are deemed worthy of benefits and the poor who are judged deserving because of their physical handicaps and advanced ages.

In 1990, the median AFDC cash grant for a single-parent family with two children was $367 per month. Because AFDC is a joint federal/state program, benefits and eligibility rules vary greatly from state to state. In January 1991, the maximum monthly AFDC grant for a family of three in Mississippi was $120, but the monthly grant was $694 in California (U.S. House of Representatives, Committee on Ways and Means 1991).

O'Hare (1987) reports that "On average, the combined value of AFDC payments and food stamps equals just 74 percent of the official poverty level. But in Alabama and Mississippi, AFDC cash payments plus food stamps provide a needy family with only 46 percent of the poverty level....The average AFDC payment per recipient in the Southern states is a little over half the average payments in the other states, after adjusting for the lower incomes in the South. In Alabama and Mississippi, per capita welfare payments are less than 5 percent of the state per capita income" (pp. 10-11).

Analysis of federal welfare expenditures from a gender perspective reveals paternalistic funding practices that give clear messages. Messages are communicated about the proper role of women in the traditional heterosexual American family structure. The woman is expected to marry a man, reproduce children, and take care of the household. If the woman works in the labor market, she has dual responsibilities in the household and on the job. Oppressive and punitive social welfare policies and marriage laws that deal with single mothers and divorced or separated women reflect the repercussions of deviating from society's norms. Socialization messages about the proper role of men extol the positive relationship between hard work and rugged individualism, success and the accumulation of money, and moral worth and materialistic signs of achievement.

Capitalist values are taught in school and reinforced in the family. Good parents are depicted as those who work long and hard to give their children material advantages. The media portrays successful American entrepreneurs as ideal role models. The majority of them are white males. While capitalism promulgates equality of opportunity for all sexes, races, and classes, growing numbers of women and minorities remain poor and disenfranchised.

Debate is ongoing whether social welfare programs should be available to all citizens or based on eligibility standards and whether benefits should be universal or means-tested. Liberals contend that the government has a moral and legal obligation to support the less fortunate, while conservatives believe that individuals should help themselves with limited assistance from private sources. This debate will continue as long as it meets the needs of special interest groups and continues to get politicians reelected. In the meantime, an expanding group of socialist feminist scholars and enlightened social welfare policy analysts are proposing a radical rethinking and comprehensive restructuring of the current American welfare state.

WOMEN AND THE WELFARE STATE

Welfare Reform

Welfare reform is a facade that has been effectively used by politicians, social welfare analysts, and government bureaucrats to divert public attention from the most critical problem facing women and children in America today. The problem is poverty. Reforming the current welfare system will not eliminate poverty because most of the poor in America do not receive federal cash welfare benefits. The majority of federal expenditures for welfare programs go to support the middle and upper classes; however, the state rarely identifies those programs as needing reform. They are supported by vocal and well organized special interest groups and powerful lobbies. When the state talks about welfare reform, it usually means tightening the eligibility standards for Aid to Families with Dependent Children, the public assistance program that supports poor mothers and young children. It also means cutting back the noncash transfer programs, such as Food Stamps and Medicaid, that supplement AFDC benefits.

Although the concept of welfare reform is an illusion, it is a popular misconception. The public views welfare reform as a long overdue means to force lazy freeloaders back to work. Social scientists who publish books and articles on welfare reform receive a great deal of media attention, and politicians relish running reelection campaigns on platforms that include welfare reform. Current proposals for welfare reform reinforce and maintain the gender and racial inequities in the existing system.

Charles Murray became the guru of welfare reform for Ronald Reagan and his conservative advisors when he published Losing Ground in 1984. He contended that government assistance programs that began during the War on Poverty encouraged the poor to remain on welfare. They reinforced dependency, discouraged work, and contributed to the rising trend in female-headed families, particularly among blacks. His proposal for welfare reform entails the elimination of all government assistance programs for the able-bodied poor of working age including AFDC, Medicaid, Food Stamps, Unemployment Insurance, Worker's Compensation, subsidized housing, and disability insurance. He labels his approach to welfare reform as "the Alexandrian solution" which is to "cut the knot, for there is no way to untie it" (Murray 1984).

Research data on trends in poverty, poverty spending, and economic performance do not support Murray's contention that increased social welfare spending that began during the 1960s has encouraged the formation of single-parent families. Since the 1970s, AFDC benefit levels have been repeatedly cut back, but family structures have continued to change. The percent of all children being raised in female-headed households increased from 12 percent to 24 percent between 1970 and 1990. During those twenty years, the percent of all children living in homes supported by AFDC benefits remained around 12 percent. The statistics for black female-headed households challenge Murray's argument even more forcefully. Between 1972 and 1980 the number of black children living in female-headed families increased almost 20 percent; however, the number of black children on AFDC decreased by 5 percent. "If AFDC were pulling families apart and encouraging the formation of single-parent families, it is hard to understand why the number of children on the program would remain constant throughout a period in our history when family structures changed the most" (Ellwood & Summers 1986, p. 94).

Murray's solution to reforming the welfare system is to have recipients get jobs. He is not suggesting a full employment strategy where the government works with the private and public sectors to create training and employment opportunities for all Americans. What Murray recommends is cutting everyone off of public assistance and literally letting them sink or swim. For a single mother on AFDC with dependent children, this solution is oppressive and sexist. It reflects an oversimplification of a very complex set of problems and issues facing women today. Because of the sexual division of labor that exists in America, most job opportunities for women are in the secondary labor market where wages are inadequate to support a family, cover health care costs, and pay for child care (Donovan 1985; Rubery 1982; Hartmann 1979; Beck, Horan & Tolbert 1978). In addition, many of these women are unskilled, undereducated, and/or illiterate. Fewer than 40 percent of all adults on AFDC are high school graduates; approximately 60 percent have math skills below the eighth or ninth grade level, and nearly half have reading skills below that level. At least one in four adults on AFDC has no prior work experience (National Coalition on Women, Work and Welfare Reform 1986, p. 3). Today's highly skilled and sexually segregated job market is not going to easily integrate women with little education, no experience, and few skills.

Another example of the illusions surrounding welfare reform is Representative Daniel Patrick Moynihan's welfare reform bill that was ratified by the U.S. Senate in 1988. This is a bill "to amend tile IV of the Social Security Act to replace the AFDC program with a comprehensive program of mandatory child support and work training which provides for transitional child care and medical assistance, benefit improvement, and mandatory extension of coverage of two- parent families, and which reflects a general emphasis on shared and reciprocal obligation, program innovation, and organizational review" (U.S. Senate 1988, Bill No. S. 1511).

Moynihan's legislation was publicized as the most significant nonpartisan welfare reform package since the War on Poverty. Whereas the bill does enhance the enforcement of child support payments and does expand welfare assistance to families where there are two parents, it also includes a mandatory work program for parents of children as young as one year at the discretion of the individual states. Similar types of welfare reform measures that require mandatory work have failed to impact on female poverty. Since 1967, the Work Incentive Program (WIN) has been the main job training and placement program for welfare recipients. "Because enrollees often needed basic education and skill training as well as child care and other supportive services, success was modest and costs were high. Indeed, even many who had successfully completed the program did not earn enough to leave the welfare rolls" (Levitan 1935, p. 120).

Since the inception of the WIN program, the number of welfare recipients trained for jobs has been small. It is estimated that "WIN moved 130,000 people off welfare in 1985, or about one percent of those on AFDC. Similarly, the much-touted, proliferating 'workfare' programs, which require recipients to work off their welfare benefits in community jobs, are believed to cover about one percent of AFDC recipients" (Whitman 1987, p. 23). Underbudgeted from the beginning and cut back during the Reagan Administration from $365 million in 1981 to $110 million in 1987, "WIN typically registers hundreds of thousands of welfare mothers who end up doing nothing, since there is no work or training available through the program" (Whitman 1987, p. 25).

The Moynihan bill provides for some work training, but history demonstrates that mandatory work programs fail because they are nothing more than seasonal and transient job placement programs that help meet the needs of capitalists for cheap labor. "In its need for low paid workers, capitalism has maintained women (and other groups) as a reserve pool of labor that can be drawn into and out of the labor force as needed. The ready availability of cheap female labor benefits capital by exerting a downward pressure on wages, while the possibility of displacement helps to keep currently employed workers in line" (Abramovitz 1988, p. 28). In addition, Moynihan's welfare reform bill contains no requirements for equal pay rates for women. For the women on AFDC, it means being forced to accept low paying service sector jobs with few benefits and no opportunities for advancement.

There is a child care provision, but it is limited to one year and pays a mere $175 a month for child care services. The bill also requires that child care be reimbursed only if it is provided at licensed day care centers. Although the number of child care centers are already insufficient to meet the current and growing demand, there are no monetary provisions in the bill to establish additional child care centers.

This is clearly a bill designed with little concern either about child care needs and costs or about the sexual division of labor. Whether a woman works twelve months or twelve years, she will not be able to afford child care services on a minimum-wage job. In 1992, a woman who works full-time at minimum wage earns $8,800 a year before taxes; this income is below the poverty threshold for a family of three which is the typical female-headed family. The national average cost of day care is $2,500 a year for 3 to 5 year olds, and the cost increases for younger children (Kamerman & Kahn 1988).

In addition to the one year child care subsidy, Moynihan's bill also subsidizes health care coverage for a maximum of twelve months. Add the cost of medical insurance to child care expenses, and you have set up an impossible financial situation for the AFDC mother. She has no other option but to quit her job and return to public assistance.

Liberal reforms of the welfare system fail to eliminate systemic inequalities faced by women and children. Welfare reform does temporarily placate taxpayers and create positive publicity for politicians; however, what is needed is the development of new models and radical strategies to combat poverty. As the National Coalition on Women, Work and Welfare Reform (1987) asserts, "The problem is poverty, not welfare. The solution to poverty is not to reduce the welfare rolls, but rather to transform the welfare system into one which enables recipients to become economically self-sufficient" (p. 1).

A Progressive Feminist Social Welfare Agenda

Elimination of poverty and restructuring the welfare system are the foci of a progressive feminist social welfare agenda. The key determinants of female poverty are jobs, wages, and levels of AFDC benefits. A minimum standard of living must be guaranteed to poor women and their dependent children who, for a variety of complex sociocultural reasons, will not be integrated into the job market. Because of gender segregation and the unequal wage structures that exist in the U.S. labor market, economic policies merit primary attention in a feminist agenda dealing with the welfare of women. Progressive economic social welfare policies that would produce long-term solutions to female poverty include full employment, comparable worth, parents' wages, tax reform, and minimum income guarantees. Family policies also need to be developed in which household labor is recognized as productive work, and wages are paid. AFDC should be eliminated and replaced with policies that provide wages to parents and allowances for children. Responsibility for child care must be shared by both genders, and the state needs to assure the availability of quality day care for all its children. A national health care policy that guarantees humane and affordable medical treatment to women and children is a necessity.

Full employment means zero unemployment among those segments of the population who are physically, mentally, and emotionally capable of working. The goal of full employment, which includes addressing the issue of substandard jobs that pay below subsistence-level salaries, would contribute significantly to the elimination of poverty among women and children. Since the Great Depression, the federal government has spent billions of dollars on job training and education programs in order to prepare the poor for the competitive job market, but they have produced few tangible results because the federal government has done little to create new job opportunities or to combat the discriminatory recruiting and hiring practices that keep women and minorities segregated in the secondary labor market.

Full employment is not a new antipoverty strategy in America. After World War II, labor lobbied for the passage of the Full Employment Bill of 1945. The Bill asserted that it was the responsibility of the federal government to guarantee that "all Americans able to work and seeking work have the right to useful, remunerative, regular and full- time employment" (Mangum 1969, p.

22). In 1975, the Hawkins-Reuss bill reintroduced legislation to guarantee full employment as a right of all adults who are capable of and desire to work in useful paid employment at fair wages (Schorr 1977). Both bills were defeated, and the prospect of guaranteeing Americans a constitutional right to a job dimmed.

Increasing numbers of social welfare policy analysts are once again reintroducing the concept of full employment as a viable strategy to eliminate poverty in America (Schorr 1977; Schiller 1984; Harrington 1984; Winpisinger 1984; Gil & Gil 1987; Abramovitz 1988). They argue that the Constitution of the United States should be amended to include a bill of economic rights. This bill would guarantee jobs and adequate wages to every person who was capable of working. Strategies for implementing a bill of economic rights include adapting the work week at periodic intervals to the needs of production and numbers of available workers, creating government-sponsored work and service projects, paying wages out of public funds to those taking care of children and disabled relatives at home (Gil 1987).

Other suggestions for implementing full employment include providing government support and subsidies to corporations that invest assets to create jobs, particularly in poverty areas. Conversely, companies that move out of financially troubled areas should have to pay for the resulting "social damage" to the area and lose all tax deductions (Harrington 1984, p. 243). Schiller (1984) suggests that we might be able to do a better job of providing jobs for the poor if we made a concerted and conscious effort to incorporate antipoverty objectives into fiscal planning. Economic policies such as increased government expenditures, consumer tax cuts, enlarged investment and depreciation allowances, and accessible credit "could move millions of persons out of poverty" (p. 192).

One of the main obstacles to full employment in America is the consciously planned use of unemployment as a means to slow inflation. The Phillips Curve is most frequently used to generalize the historical relationship between lower rates of unemployment and higher rates of inflation. Since inflation impacts more on the wealthy than the poor, the government chooses to sacrifice the jobs of the middle and lower classes rather than the profits of capitalists. Winpisinger (1984) finds this policy indefensible and argues for "controls on prices, profits and incomes derived from sources other than labor" (p. 21). Focusing on women, Abramovitz (1988) argues that "A labor market policy that assured employment, training or retraining for all those able to work, that set the minimum wage to automatically keep pace with changes in the standard of living, and that tolerated neither unemployment as a means to check inflation nor discrimination of any kind would go far towards assuring that women would rely on jobs rather than AFDC" (p. 367).

Full employment would lower poverty rates among women and children. Jobs alone, however, would not eliminate poverty because many women work and are still poor. For women, effective antipoverty strategies must address discriminatory hiring practices that assign women to "female jobs" in the secondary labor market that pay minimum or below subsistence-level wages and provide no benefits. In addition, strategies must challenge discriminatory salary practices that pay women different wages than men for the same or comparable work. Women earn approximately 70 percent of what men earn, and there are few encouraging signs that this gap is diminishing. Regardless of whether women work in professional careers, in retail, or in service jobs, their earnings are less than men. A little less than 40 percent of the professional fields are comprised of women; they earn 71.2 percent of what men earn. Women working in retail are 60 percent of the work force, yet they earn only 67.4 percent of what men earn. In service sector jobs in which women make up 78.4 percent of the labor force, they still earn only 67 percent of what men earn (Sidel 1986).

Identifying and implementing strategies to combat sexist wage structures in the labor market contribute significantly to reducing poverty among women and the children they are responsible for supporting. One of the most controversial strategies is comparable worth.

Comparable worth proposes giving equal pay for work of comparable value. It achieved national attention in 1979 during the administration of Jimmy Carter. He selected a woman, Eleanor Holmes Norton, to be Chair of the Equal Employment Opportunity Commission, and she formed a national committee to examine the feasibility of implementing a comparable worth policy. Comparable worth challenges the historical pattern of paying lower wages to workers in occupations that are categorized as "female."

Proponents of comparable worth believe that discrimination against women contributes to lower wage scales in jobs that are identified as "female," so they support a strategy of wage scale adjustments (Hartmann, Roos, & Treiman 1985; Amott & Matthaei 1986). Implementing a policy of comparable worth entails detailed preparation and arduous negotiation. It requires careful research of job performance evaluation systems and unbiased procedures for describing and rating jobs performed by men and women. This involves evaluating the bases of the wage scales for positions held predominantly by men and those held predominantly by women. After examination of job descriptions and discussion with workers, attempts are then made to establish objective criteria for job components such as level of skill, job responsibility, amount of work effort required, and working conditions. Jobs are usually ranked on a value scale in which points are assigned to each job according to objective criteria. Dollar values are then assigned to the points, and wages are realigned accordingly.

In addition to being complex, a comparable worth strategy threatens the economic power base of the business world. A policy of comparable worth would not only redistribute income to women, it would also shift power to women workers in the U.S. labor market that has always been controlled by male interests. In reality, the adoption of a comparable worth policy will take many years; nevertheless, it belongs on a feminist agenda attempting to combat the pauperization of women.

Another progressive social welfare policy that would improve the economic circumstances of women and mark progress toward the formulation of a comprehensive family policy in the United States is parents' wages. Some policy planners support the concept of mothers' wages which would pay wages to every mother and expectant mother during periods in which they were not in the labor market because of childbearing and childrearing responsibilities. Such a proposal is sexist and based on the erroneous assumption that it is the woman who is solely responsible for household tasks including child care. The literature documents that women's responsibility for housework and child care negatively correlates with labor market participation and income (Cowan 1987; Smith 1987; Berk 1980; Malos 1980). Economic equality for women not only entails better jobs and higher wages but also shared responsibility with men for household tasks and child care. Regardless of whether it is the man or woman performing domestic tasks, the work merits reimbursement.

Parents' wages would be paid to mothers and/or fathers who choose to care for their children at home. They would be paid the equivalent of one full-time salary. The amount would be established by the Bureau of Labor Statistics and guarantee a decent standard of living. This salary would be supported by tax revenues and be equivalent to the wages of child care workers in federally supported day care centers. Comprehensive and universal child care services would be an integral part of this program. Parents from all socioeconomic classes would be eligible to receive wages for household labor and to utilize government supported child care centers. The initial federal investment of revenue in a program of parents' wages would be significant; projected costs, which include the establishment of child care centers, are estimated at $50 billion. These costs, however, lessen over time as increasing numbers of both fathers and mothers work outside the home and need child care services.

Another concern is that a policy of parents' wages does not address the economic needs of impoverished families without children under 18 years of age. This factor makes it imperative to include a minimum income guarantee program in a progressive feminist social welfare agenda. It is discriminatory and sexist to establish antipoverty policies that assist only those families that uphold the traditional American values of marriage and the family.

The implementation of a program of parents' wages requires a reconceptualization of child care and housework as useful and productive labor. Up to now, capitalism has defined productive work as work that produces surplus value for the profit of the owners of the means of production. It also would require Americans to begin accepting social welfare services as universal rights that are equally available to all regardless of class, gender, or race. Gil (1973) predicts "strong resistance" to a policy of parents' wages from political groups "committed to the preservation of the existing social order and its value premises and ideology" (p. 130).

Few governmental policies support the existing economic structure more effectively than the American system of taxation. The typical wealthy families are those whose annual incomes are over a half million dollars a year. They pay more than one-quarter less of their incomes in combined income, property, and sales taxes than do middle-income families who earn about $27,000 a year and poor families who earn less than $7,600 a year. Wealthy families pay approximately 5.1 percent of their income in state and local taxes, while a poor family pays around 7 percent (McIntyre et al. 1987).

Tax reform needs to be included on a progressive feminist antipoverty agenda because the current regressive system of taxation overburdens the working poor, marginal workers who move in and out of the work force, and part-time workers. Large numbers of women supporting dependent children fall into one of these three categories. Progressive tax reform measures would provide incentives for poor and low-income women to enter and remain in the labor market not punish them by disproportionately taxing their income more than the income of the wealthy. The following analysis relies heavily on the writings of Sheldon Danziger, former Director of the Institute for Research on Poverty at the University of Wisconsin in Madison, who is one of the country's foremost social work scholars on poverty.

In 1975, Congress approved the earned income tax credit (EITC) to subsidize the earnings of low-income families with children. Over a ten year period, inflation eroded the federal tax credit of $250 for a family of four at the poverty line; the same family now pays $370 in income taxes. That amounts to an increase in taxes of $620 for that poor family. The Tax Reform Act of 1986 increased the standard deduction, the personal exemption, and the EITC and indexed them to inflation. By 1990 the reforms were implemented and reduced some of the tax burdens of the poor.

These latest tax reforms are not sufficient, however, to counteract the rising poverty rates in America due to "adverse market forces and reductions in income transfers that have characterized the period since 1973." Danziger (1987) suggests two additional income tax reforms that would aid the working poor and prevent them from needing public assistance:

> 1. A per capita refundable credit to replace the personal exemption. This credit would target more forgone revenue on those with lower incomes than would an increase in the personal exemption. A per capita refundable credit could be made high enough to replace both the personal exemption and the food stamp program.
> 2. A refundable child-care tax credit. The
> current nonrefundable credit allows couples, when both spouses work, as well as working single parents, to subtract from their taxes a proportion of their work-related child-care costs. Very few poor families make use of this credit, however, because they do not have enough positive income tax liability to offset any refund to which they are entitled. (p. 15)

Danziger's suggestions reflect a growing trend among enlightened social welfare policy analysts to concentrate on broad and universal antipoverty proposals rather than on narrow and antiquated visions of welfare reform. There will always be a need for some type of minimum income guarantee program in America to protect the dignity and rights of those incapable of providing for themselves. Whether these individuals be young or old, male or female, mentally retarded or physically impaired, emotionally disturbed or educationally handicapped, all Americans have the right to live at a basic decent standard of living.

On the other hand, aggressive antipoverty strategies need to be developed to help those struggling to survive without the help of the public assistance programs. Low-income families often require some type of economic intervention in order to remain off the welfare rolls. Implementing tax credits and other tax reforms to help low- income families is a positive step toward redirecting governmental antipoverty efforts away from punitive and sexist means-tested public assistance programs. As Lerman (1988) asserts, "...the nonwelfare strategy is a low-cost way to reduce poverty while reorienting the income support system away from welfare programs" (p. 28).

In addition to economic policies, a progressive feminist antipoverty agenda must include family policies that eliminate the iniquitous treatment of women and address the needs of children. Children are in crisis in America; growing numbers are hungry, homeless, neglected, and abused. Because low-income working parents cannot afford child care, increasing numbers of children are left alone to care for themselves and younger siblings. Others are left with inexperienced baby-sitters or neighbors willing to watch the children in order to earn a few extra dollars. Two policies that would impact positively on the care of children and help relieve some of the financial pressures burdening parents, many of whom are single women, are children's allowances and child care services.

Children's allowances are a universal social welfare program that provide monthly grants to all families regardless of income or family structure. Every Western industrialized country except the United States has some kind of comprehensive family policy that provides children's allowances. Depending on the country, amounts of the allowances vary by the number and ages of the children and usually are larger for single-parent families. Although the size of the grants is relatively small, they significantly help low-income families, in particular, single-parent families (Kamerman 1984). Supporters of children's allowances argue that even a minimal level of financial security promotes a more positive family environment in which children are given opportunities to grow and prosper.

The purpose of children's allowances is to alleviate some of the financial burdens of raising children. A factor that contributes to higher poverty rates is number of children in the family. Studies have shown that when heads of households work full-time and earn minimum wage, they are unable to keep a family with three or more dependents from poverty. Likewise, the maximum family benefit in the lowest wage bracket of social security provides only enough income to support the insured and one dependent (Ozawa 1977).

There is a particularly significant correlation between number of children and poverty for single women raising children. Rodgers (1986) reports that "In 1984, for example, 33.3 percent of all female household heads with one child were poor, rising to 66 percent of those with three children, and 79 percent of those with four children. The poverty rates for minority women were even higher. Fifty-seven percent of all black female family heads with two children lived in poverty" (p. 44). In addition, studies have shown that women with two or more children have higher rates of unemployment, lower employment and career aspirations, and lower incomes (Smith-Loving and Tickamyer 1982).

Implementation of a children's allowance program would undoubtedly face similar obstacles to those encountered in attempting to implement a program of parents' wages. Costs of a children's allowance program would be paid out of federal revenues; however, government outlay would be offset by requiring that allowances be taxed as part of yearly income and implementing a progressive tax reform system that would redistribute income from the upper to the lower classes. In addition, most itemized deductions and the personal exemptions in the current tax system would be replaced by per capita tax credits with a modest income guarantee built into the proposal (Gil 1987; Danziger 1986).

Another component of a progressive feminist family policy is comprehensive and universal child care services. Child care services are critically needed in America. Poor women, who have always had to work in order to support their children, have known this for decades but have had no power to influence policy making. Now that women of all classes are joining the labor force, lack of child care services is beginning to receive attention.

During World War II, the federal government became involved in providing child care services; the Lanham Act authorized federal funds to support day care centers for mothers working in defense plants. Once the war was over, child care funds were withdrawn. Women were laid off, so men could return to work, and women could return to their "rightful" place in the home to cook, clean, and care for children.

The Department of Health and Human Services currently provides some federal monies for child care services for AFDC mothers, but there are many problems with the program in its current form. There are not enough quality day care centers available to low-income mothers, and the federal reimbursement rate for child care fees is not adequate to cover actual costs. In addition, child care benefits are usually extended for only three months after an AFDC mother gets a job. After that period of time, women have to pay for child care out of their earnings. The working poor simply cannot afford child care costs. The result is that only about 10 percent of the nation's 11 million poor children receive any type of day-care assistance. Furthermore, some of the child care services available to the poor simply provide custodial care rather than quality day care (Rodgers 1982).

Lack of affordable child care services is not just an issue for poor women. As women from all classes enter the labor market in increasing numbers, the child care crisis impacts on men and women from all socioeconomic backgrounds. In 1984, "almost half of all mothers with children under three and almost 52 percent of mothers with children under six were in the labor force. More than 9 million children under six have working mothers, and 67 percent of these mothers work full time" (Blank 1984, p. 7). For this reason, licensed child care services of high quality should be supported by the federal government and offered to all citizens regardless of income level.

When discussing the expense of implementing universal child care services, a cost factor analysis must be included that compares government expenditures for preventive services versus outlays for treatment programs. It is far less costly to support early childhood programs that foster positive sociopsychological development and teach educational skills to young children than it is to build juvenile prisons, finance adolescent chemical dependency rehabilitation programs, and fund adolescent psychiatric clinics. A recent study of the Children's Defense Fund reports that "A continuum of investment in prenatal care, preventive health care through age eighteen, Head Start, Chapter 1 Compensatory Education, summer jobs for the high school years, and four years of public college paid at public expense adds up to less than $39,000 for a child. That equals what seventeen months of prison costs per inmate--the average time served for a first conviction is 15.9 months. A year in prison costs $28,000" (Streit 1988).

As the discussion and analysis of a feminist social welfare agenda progresses, the need for comprehensive and integrative program planning and implementation is apparent. The success of one program usually hinges on the implementation of another. A full employment strategy entails building into the system a minimum income guarantee program to assist those incapable of working. A truly progressive full employment agenda includes a program of parents' wages that subsidizes parents for doing housework and providing child care in the home. If both parents want or need to work outside the home, comprehensive and universal child care services need to be a part of an effective full employment strategy. Full employment means addressing the issue of pay inequity for women by implementing a comparable worth campaign. The effectiveness of these strategies is augmented by reforming the current regressive tax system.

One last program that must be included on a feminist antipoverty agenda is a national health care policy that ensures humane and affordable medical treatment to all citizens regardless of class, gender, race, or age. Universal health care is "a comprehensive, high quality, federally funded, and locally controlled health maintenance system that would be established to provide preventive and curative health care for everyone. It would replace the existing, wasteful, discriminatory and totally inadequate and irrational medical care system including Medicaid, Medicare, private practice for fees, and private and public fragmentary insurance schemes" (Gil 1987, p. 56).

In America, national health insurance has been resisted since the time of the Depression. A system of national health insurance was part of the original New Deal legislation, but Franklin D. Roosevelt withdrew the proposal when strong opposition from powerful lobbies threatened to block passage of his entire social security package. Those interest groups, which stood to lose huge profits, included business, the insurance industry, and the medical profession.

Quality of the delivery of health care services in America is increasingly linked to one's ability to pay or to one's income bracket. More money ensures access to better medical treatment, more available ancillary health services, and more highly specialized doctors. Lack of money means no health care coverage whatsoever and little, if any, utilization of the health care delivery system. The number of people under age sixty-five who report lack of medical insurance increased from 28.7 million in 1979 to 32.7 million or 16 percent of the population in 1982. This represents a 15 percent increase in uninsured Americans in just three years. In 1982, 11.6 million people without health insurance had incomes below the poverty level, and another 9.6 million without insurance had incomes between 100 and 200 percent of the poverty level. These two groups combined accounted for two-thirds of the uninsured in America (Swartz 1984).

In 1992, thirty-seven million Americans or approximately one in eight are uninsured and millions more underinsured. Those particularly affected by health care costs are the working poor or families on the margin of economic security. Often these marginal workers are single women trying to juggle the costs of supporting a household with dependent children and paying for medical care needs. According to Schiller (1984), "Such families are likely to be ill more often and less likely to be protected by insurance. Consequently, they are prone to fall into poverty when illness strikes. Near-poor families do, in fact, move back and forth across the poverty line with great frequency. In part, this movement is due to the sporadic occurrence of illness" (p. 84).

All major western European industrialized nations have a system of national health insurance except the United States. The way that national health insurance programs most typically work is that participants are enrolled through their employer who is required to participate in an approved health insurance plan. Part of the cost of the program is supported by health insurance fees that are paid every month by the employer and employee. Those not covered through work, such as the elderly or unemployed, are supported by the government. Participants select their own doctors who charge fees for their services, but the government establishes the reimbursement rates rather than the doctors themselves.

The rising cost of health care in America is astounding; twelve percent of the Gross National Product (GNP) is spent on health care. Both privately supported and publicly financed systems are struggling to keep up with escalating costs. Most male workers and their families are covered through personnel benefits at work. A large group of transitory and part-time workers in the secondary labor market receive no health care benefits with their jobs; these are predominantly women with dependent children. Their low wages give them no financial cushion to absorb medical expenses. As a result, preventive medicine is not affordable, so medical treatment by crisis becomes the norm for low-income families. Delivery of health care services to the poor on a crisis intervention model is ineffective cost wise, but much more importantly, it permits a higher incidence of sickness, disease, and death in certain groups in the population because of factors relating to class, gender, and race.

The rising cost of government-supported health care programs also has many policy analysts and government leaders worried. In 1988, Medicare and Medicaid cost the federal government $114 billion dollars which represents 22 percent of total federal welfare budget expenditures (see Table 6). Health function spending in constant dollars rose 330 percent between 1966 and 1985 from $8 billion to $34 billion (U.S. Library of Congress 1986).

There is a clear need for the implementation of a national health care plan. If the experiences from other western industrialized countries can be applied to America, the government costs for supporting universal health care are comparable to the current system. More important than budgetary considerations, however, is the shameful fact that in the richest industrialized nation in the world, there are large segments of the population who remain sick and untreated or who die unnecessarily simply because they are the wrong class, gender, or race.

STRATEGIES FOR SOCIAL CHANGE

There is a lack of adequate financial resources for women in America. The numbers of poor women and children are steadily rising, yet many of them do not receive benefits from the federal income transfer social welfare programs. Tedious local bureaucratic procedures discourage potential recipients, rigid and restrictive local welfare policies and procedures make them ineligible, potential recipients oftentimes are unaware that they have the right to welfare benefits, or they simply are made to feel too ashamed or embarrassed to apply. Women and children who do receive public assistance benefits are in the transfer programs that have experienced the most drastic cutbacks and are currently undergoing the most punitive "reforms." The data presented support the fact that many women and children are in a crisis situation and that social welfare policies have not effectively addressed their needs.

The social welfare system is based on an antiquated and poorly conceived model established in the midst of the Great Depression to quell the rising discontent of unemployed males. America is the only major industrialized country in the Western world that does not have comprehensive social welfare policies that focus on the needs of the family, particularly in relation to women, work, and child care. America is the only major industrialized country in the world that has failed to implement a national health care plan.

The configuration of programs and services in the American welfare state needs to be dramatically altered. Guided by feminist values, restructuring the welfare system must be accomplished through shared rather than hierarchical decision-making. Changes need to be implemented through cooperation and consensus, not through the traditional male strategies of domination and competition. The focus of a progressive feminist social welfare agenda is not only the empowerment of individuals but the modification of societal structures that inhibit full and equal participation regardless of class, gender, or race. Both process and outcome are valued in the feminist struggle for change.

Political and economic systems do not change readily. Systemic change is a painstakingly slow process. The most revolutionary feminists continually struggle for social justice and racial and gender equality against the powerful capitalist patriarchal power structure. These women do not give up in the face of seemingly insurmountable odds and refuse to be coopted by the money and status of the power elite. These women, and some men, often work quietly yet effectively to develop alternative family and community structures that are free of gender, race, and class biases. These women organize the voices of opposition in neighborhoods, schools, churches, political parties, universities, cities, and work places when those in power continue to establish and support discriminatory policies and procedures. These women lobby for legislative changes, run for political offices at all levels of government, and consistently vote for politicians who support women's rights. These feminists are the ones who no longer accept the facade of short-term and ineffectual welfare reform but offer genuine long-range antipoverty strategies that will eliminate poverty and not simply mask its symptoms.

Caution must be taken not to confuse the progress made by individual women with legitimate systemic change. The accomplishments of women, who are breaking through corporate, educational, and political barriers that have previously excluded women from a wide variety of occupations and professions, are impressive. Using this highly visible group of women, however, as the measure of progress of women in general is deceptive because they are a minority. They are predominantly from the upper classes and mostly white. This does not make them villains; it makes them unique. The problem is that the male hierarchy uses these women as symbols that gender equality does truly exist if one only tries hard enough. If some women can make it, then all can. Failure to find employment or to remain off welfare reflect personal inadequacies.

Socialist feminists need to change the language of the discourse and the rules of the game. It must be demonstrated that it is sexist and racist social welfare institutions and structures that create poverty not individual characteristics and deficiencies. Alternative institutions and programs such as cooperative day care centers, women's health clinics, and family policies that reflect an acceptance of diverse lifestyles and shared parental responsibilities need to be established. Based on the principles of cooperation, shared decision-making, and redistribution of fiscal resources, strategies must be implemented for full employment, comparable worth, and tax reform.

Socialist feminists need to show government leaders that political rhetoric and liberal welfare reform ideologies are not acceptable. Long-term antipoverty policy planning needs to be undertaken. The middle- and upper-class feminist agenda needs to be broadened to include the social welfare needs and concerns of impoverished women and women of color. Socialist feminists must identify new strategies to educate the public and, in particular, other women about the critical issues and problems facing large numbers of low-income women and their children.

Genuine social change will occur when a united front of women and men of all classes, races, and ages works cooperatively to implement a progressive feminist social welfare agenda that upholds the dignity of every person by guaranteeing a minimal standard of living and health care and by establishing policies of equal income, opportunity, and reimbursement in the labor market and in the household. A feminist agenda creates a humane and just society in which women and men, people of color and whites, young and old experience social, political, and economic equality. This is the promise of democracy; this is the vision of the feminist movement.

BIBLIOGRAPHY

Abramovitz, M. (1986). Social policy and the female pauper: The family ethic and the U.S. welfare state. In N. V. D. Bergh & L. B. Cooper (Eds.), Feminist visions for social work (pp. 211-228). Silver Spring, MD: National Association of Social Workers.

Abramovitz, M. (1988). Regulating the lives of women. Boston, MA: South End Press.

Alexander, C. A., & Weber, D. N. (1978). Distinctive dates in social welfare history: A Chronological listing. Washington, DC: National Association of Social Workers.

Amott, T., & Matthaei, J. (1986). Comparable worth, incomparable pay. In R. Lefkowitz & A. Withorn (Eds.), For crying out loud women and poverty in the United States (pp. 316-325). New York: The Pilgrim Press.

Atkinson, T. (1974). Amazon odyssey. New York: Links Books.

Axinn, J., & Levin, H. (1975). Social welfare a history of the American response to need. New York: Dodd, Mead & Company.

Barrett, M. (1980). Women's oppression today: Problems in Marxist feminist analysis. London: Verso.

Beauvoir, S. de. (1953). The second sex. New York: Alfred A. Knopf.

Beck, E. M., Horan, P. M., & Tolbert, C. M. (1978). Stratification in a dual economy: A sectoral model of earnings determination. American Sociological Review, 43, 704-720.

Bell, W. (1965). Aid to dependent children. New York: Columbia University Press.

Benston, M. (1969). The political economy of women's liberation. Monthly Review, 21(4), 13-27.

Berk, S. F. (Ed.). (1980). Women and household labor. Beverly Hills: Sage Publications.

Berk, S. F. (1985). The gender factory. New York: Plenum Press.

Blank, H. (1984). Child care: The states' response: A survey of state child care policies, 1983-1984 (White paper). Washington, DC: Children's Defense Fund.

Burnham, L. (1986). Has poverty been feminized in black America?. In R. Lefkowitz & A. Withorn (Eds.), For crying out loud women and poverty in the United States (pp. 69-83). New York: The Pilgrim Press.

Burtless, G. (1986). Public spending for the poor: Trends, prospects, and economic limits. In S. H. Danziger & D. H. Weinberg (Eds.), Fighting poverty what works and what doesn't (pp. 18-49). Cambridge, MA: Harvard University Press.

Chodorow, N. (1978). The reproduction of mothering: Psychoanalysis and the sociology of gender. Berkeley: University of California Press.

Coverman, S. (1983). Gender, domestic labor time, and wage inequality. American Sociological Review, 48, 623-637.

Cowan, R. S. (1987). Women's work, housework, and history: The historical roots of inequality in work-force participation. In N. Gerstel & H. E. Gross (Eds.), Families and work (pp. 164-177). Philadelphia: Temple University Press.

Dalla Costa, M., & James, S. (1980). The power of women and the subversion of the community. In E. Malos (Ed.), The politics of housework (pp. 160-195). London: Allison & Busby.

Danziger, S. H. (1987). The antipoverty significance of the Tax Reform Act of 1986. Focus, 10, 15.

Danziger, S. H., & Weinberg, D. H. (Eds.). (1986). Fighting poverty what works and what doesn't. Cambridge, MA: Harvard University Press.

Dickenson, K. (1975). Transfer income. In Five thousand families: Patterns of economic progress, Vol. 1. Ann Arbor: University of Michigan Survey Research Center.

Donovan, J. (1985). Feminist theory the intellectual traditions of American feminism. New York: Frederick Ungar.

Duncan, G. J., & Corcoran, M. E. (1984). Do women "deserve" to earn less than men?. In G. J. Duncan (Ed.), Years of poverty years of plenty (pp. 153-180). The University of Michigan: Institute for Social Research.

Economic Report of the President: 1973. (1973). Washington, DC: U. S. Government Printing Office.

Eisenstein, Z. (1979a). Capitalist patriarchy and the case for socialist feminism. New York: Monthly Review Press.

Eisenstein, Z. (1979b). Developing a theory of capitalist patriarchy and socialist feminism. In Z. Eisenstein (Ed.), Capitalist patriarchy and the case for socialist feminism (pp. 5-40). New York: Monthly Review Press.

Eisenstein, Z. (1981). The radical future of liberal feminism. New York: Longman.

Ellwood, D. T., & Summers, L. H. (1986). Poverty in America: Is welfare the answer or the problem?. In S. H. Danziger & D. H. Weinberg (Eds.), Fighting poverty what works and what doesn't (pp. 78-105). Cambridge, MA: Harvard University Press.

Engels, F. (1942) The origin of the family, private property and the state. New York: International.

England, P. (1982). The failure of human capital theory to explain occupational sex segregation. The Journal of Human Resources, 17, 358-370.

Firestone, S. (1970). The dialectic of sex the case for feminist revolution. New York: William Morrow.

Folbre, N. (1987). The pauperization of motherhood: Patriarchy and public policy in the United States. In N. Gerstel & H. E. Gross (Eds.), Families and work (pp. 491-511). Philadelphia: Temple University Press.

Galper, J. H. (1975). The politics of social services. Englewood Cliffs, NJ: Prentice-Hall.

Germain, C. B., & Hartman, A. (1980). People and ideas in the history of social work practice. Social Casework, 61, 323-331.

Gil, D. G. (1973). Unravelling social policy theory, analysis, and political action towards social equality. Cambridge, MA: Schenkman.

Gil, D. G. (1987). Book review: Women and children last. Catalyst: A Socialist Journal Of The Social Services, 6(1), 53-57.

Gil, D. G., & Gil, E. A. (Eds.) (1987). The future of work. Cambridge, MA: Schenkman.

Glazer, N. (1980). Everyone needs three hands: Doing unpaid and paid work. In S. F. Berk (Ed.), Women and household labor (pp. 249-273). Beverly Hills: Sage.

Gorham, W. (1984). Overview. In D. L. Bawden (Ed.), The social contract revisited aims and outcomes of President Reagan's social welfare policy. (pp. 1-14). Washington, DC: Urban Institute Press.

Greer, G. (1971). The female eunich. New York: McGraw Hill.

Hampton, R. (1975). Marital dissolution: Some social and economic consequences. In *Five thousand families: Patterns of economic progress, Vol. 3*. Ann Arbor: University of Michigan Survey Research Center.

Harrington, M. (1984). *The new American poverty*. New York: Penguin Books.

Hartmann, H. (1979). Capitalism, patriarchy and job segregation by sex. In Z. Eisenstein (Ed.), *Capitalist patriarchy and the case for socialist feminism* (pp. 206-247). New York: Monthly Review Press.

Hartmann, H. (1981). The unhappy marriage of Marxism and feminism. In L. Sargent (Ed.), *Woman and revolution* (pp. 1-41). Boston: South End.

Hartmann, H., Roos, P., & Treiman, D. (1985). An agenda for basic research on comparable worth. In H. Hartmann (Ed.), *Comparable worth new directions for research* (pp. 3-33). Washington, DC: National Academy Press.

Higginbotham, E. (1986). We were never on a pedestal women of color continue to struggle with poverty, racism, and sexism. In R. Lefkowitz & A. Withorn (Eds.), *For crying out loud women and poverty in the United States* (pp. 99-110). New York: The Pilgrim Press.

Jaggar, A. M. (1983). *Feminist politics and human nature*. Totowa, NJ: Rowman & Allanheld.

Kamerman, S. B. (1984). Women, children and poverty: public policies and female-headed families in industrialized countries. *Signs: Journal of Women in Culture and Society, 10*, 249-271.

Kamerman, S. B., & Kahn, A. J. (1988). *Mothers alone strategies for a time of change*. Dover, MA: Auburn House.

Katz, M. B. (1986). *In the shadow of the poorhouse a social history of welfare in America*. New York: Basic Books.

Katznelson, I., & Kesselman, M. (1987). The politics of power a critical introduction to American government. New York: Harcourt Brace Jovanovich.

Kelly, J. (1984). Women, history & theory. Chicago: The University of Chicago Press.

King v. Smith, 392, U. S. Supreme Court 309 (1963).

Lenski, G. E. (1966). Power and privilege: A theory of social stratification. New York: McGraw-Hill.

Lerman, R. I. (1988). Nonwelfare approaches to helping the poor. Focus, 11, 24-28.

Levitan, S. A. (1985). Programs in aid of the poor. Baltimore: The John Hopkins University Press.

Malos, E. (Ed.). (1980). The politics of housework. London: Allison & Busby.

Mangum, G. (1969). The emergence of manpower policy. New York: Holt, Rinehart, and Winston.

Marx, K. (1918). Capital. London: William Glaisher.

Marx, K. (1964). The economic and philosophic manuscripts of 1844. New York: International Publishers.

Marx, K., & Engels, F. (1966). The Communist Manifesto. New York: Washington Square Press.

McIntyre, R. S., Wilhelm, D., Spinner, J., Anzalone, J., Forrer, J., & Sika, D. (1987). The sorry state of state taxes and the golden opportunity of federal tax reform. Washington, DC: Citizens for Tax Justice.

Meyer, C. H. (1970). Social work practice: A response to the urban crisis. New York: The Free Press.

Meyer, J. A. (1984). Budget cuts in the Reagan Administration: A question of fairness. In D. L. Bawden (Ed.), The social contract revisited (pp. 33-64). Washington, DC: Urban Institute Press.

Millett, K. (1970). Sexual politics. Garden City, NY: Doubleday.

Mitchell, J. (1971). Woman's estate. New York: Pantheon Books.

Murray, C. (1984). Losing ground American social policy 1950-1980. New York: Basic Books.

National Coalition on Women, Work and Welfare Reform. (1986). Perspectives on women and welfare employment. Washington, DC: Wider Opportunities for Women.

National Coalition on Women, Work and Welfare Reform. (1987). Changing welfare: An investment in women and children in poverty. Washington, DC: Wider Opportunities for Women.

O'Hare, W. P. (1985). Poverty in America: Trends and new patterns. Population Bulletin. (Vol. 40, No. 3). Washington, DC: Population Reference Bureau.

O'Hare, W. P. (1987). America's welfare population: Who gets what?. Population trends and public policy. (No. 13). Washington, DC: Population Reference Bureau.

Ozawa, M. N. (1977). Social insurance and redistribution. In A. L. Schorr (Ed.), Jubilee for our times a practical program for income equality (pp. 123-177). New York: Columbia University Press.

Parrish v. The Civil Service Commission of the County of Alameda, S. F., 22429, Supreme Court of California in Bank (1967, March 27).

Pearce, D. (1986). The feminization of poverty women, work, and welfare. In R. Lefkowitz & A. Withorn (Eds.), For crying out loud women and poverty in the United States (pp. 29-46). New York: The Pilgrim Press.

Piven, F. F., & Cloward. R. A. (1971). Regulating the poor: The functions of public welfare. New York: Vintage Books.

Piven, F. F., & Cloward, R. A. (1982). The new class war Reagan's attack on the welfare state and its consequences. New York: Pantheon Books.

Polachek, S. (1979). Occupational segregation among women: theory, evidence, and a prognosis. In C. Lloyd, E. Andrews, & C. Gilroy (Eds.), Women in the labor market (pp. 137-157). New York: Columbia University Press.

Proceedings of the White House Conference On Children. (1909, January). Washington, DC.

Report of the Committee on Economic Security. (1935, January 15). Reprinted in 50th anniversary issue, the report of the committee on economic security of 1935 and other basic documents relating to the Social Security Act. Washington, DC: National Conference on Social Welfare, 1985.

Rodgers, H. R., Jr. (1982). The cost of human neglect America's welfare failure. Armonk, NY: M. E. Sharpe.

Rodgers, H. R., Jr. (1986). Poor women, poor families the economic plight of America's female-headed households. Armonk, NY: M. E. Sharpe.

Rubery, J. (1982). Structured labour markets, worker organisation, and low pay. In A. Giddens & D. Held (Eds.), Classes, power, and conflict (pp. 330-348). Berkeley: University of California Press.

Ryan, W. (1971). Blaming the victim. New York: Vintage Books.

Sacks, K. (1979). *Sisters and wives the past and future of sexual equality.* Westport, CT: Greenwood Press.

Schiller, B. R. (1984). *The economics of poverty and discrimination.* Englewood Cliffs, NJ: Prentice-Hall.

Schorr, A. L. (Ed.). (1977). *Jubilee for our times a practical program for income equality.* New York: Columbia University Press.

Sidel, R. (1986). *Women and children last the plight of poor women in affluent America.* New York: Viking.

Smith, D. E. (1987). Women's inequality and the family. In N. Gerstel & H. E. Gross (Eds.), *Families and work* (pp. 23-54). Philadelphia: Temple University Press.

Smith-Loving, L., & Tickamyer, A. (1982). Models of fertility and women's work. *American Sociological Review, 47,* 561-566.

Sokoloff, N. J. (1980). *Between money and love the dialectics of women's home and market work.* New York: Praeger.

Streit, P. (Ed.). (1988, May). *Monthly Report on Poverty and Hunger in America.* (Available from Hunger Action Forum, 1717 Massachusetts Avenue, N.W., Suite 604, Washington, DC 20036)

Swartz, K. (1984). *The changing face of the uninsured.* Paper presented at the first annual meeting of the Association for Health Service Researchers, Washington, DC.

Trattner, W. I. (1979). *From poor law to welfare state.* New York: The Free Press.

U.S. Bureau of the Census. (1983). Money income, 1983. *Current population reports.* Washington, DC: U.S. Government Printing Office.

U.S. Bureau of the Census. (1985). Money income and poverty status of families and persons in the United States: 1984. Current population reports. (Series P- 60, No. 149). Washington, DC: U.S. Government Printing Office.

U.S. Bureau of the Census. (1991). Poverty in the United States: 1990. Current population reports. (Series P-60, No. 175). Washington, DC: U.S. Government Printing Office.

U.S. Congress. House of Representatives. (1962). Compilation of the Social Security laws, including the Social Security Act, as amended, and related enactments. (No. 616, 87th Congress, 2nd session). Washington, DC.: U.S. Government Printing Office.

U.S. Department of Health, Education, and Welfare. Social Security Administration. (1961, monthly). Social Security Bulletin. Washington, DC: U.S. Government Printing Office.

U.S. Department of Health and Human Services. Social Security Administration. (May 1991). Social Security Bulletin. Washington, DC: U.S. Government Printing Office.

U.S. House of Representatives. Committee on Ways and Means. (1985). Background material and data on programs within the jurisdiction of the Committee on Ways and Means. (No. 99-2). Washington, DC: U.S. Government Printing Office.

U.S. House of Representatives. Committee on Ways and Means. (1991). Background material and data on programs within the jurisdiction of the Committee on Ways and Means. (Table 7). Washington, DC: U.S. Government Printing Office.

U.S. Library of Congress. Congressional Research Service. (1986). 1987 Budget perspectives: federal spending for the human resource programs. (Report No. 86-46 EPW, by G. Falk). Washington, DC: U.S. Government Printing Office.

U.S. Library of Congress. Congressional Research Service. (1989). <u>Cash and noncash benefits for persons with limited income: Eligibility rules, recipient and expenditure date, FY 1986-88.</u> (Report No. 89-595). Washington, DC: U.S. Government Printing Office.

U.S. Office of Management and Budget. Congressional Research Service. (1985). <u>Historical tables: Budget of the United States Government, fiscal year 1986.</u> Washington, DC: U.S. Government Printing Office.

U.S. Office of Management and Budget. Congressional Research Service. (1989). <u>Historical tables: Budget of the United States Government, fiscal year 1990.</u> Washington, DC: U.S. Government Printing Office.

U.S. Senate. 100th Congress. 1st Session. (1988). <u>Bill No. S. 1511</u>. Washington, DC: U.S. Government Printing Office.

Ware, S. (1981). <u>Beyond suffrage women in the New Deal</u>. Cambridge, MA: Harvard University Press.

Webb, S., & Webb, B. (1927). <u>English local government: English poor law history</u>. New York: Longmans.

Whitman, D. (1987, June). The key to welfare reform. <u>The Atlantic</u>, pp. 22-25.

Wilensky, H. L., & Lebeaux, C. N. (1965). <u>Industrial society and social welfare.</u> New York: The Free Press.

Winpisinger, W. W. (1984). Rebuilding America with full employment. <u>Socialist Review,</u> 14(3 & 4), 16-24.

Withorn, A. (1985). The forced choice: Making change vs. helping people. In D. G. Gil & E. A. Gil (Eds.), <u>Toward social and economic justice</u> (pp. 3-37). Cambridge, MA: Schenkman Publishing.

APPENDIX

U.S. FEDERAL GOVERNMENT ASSISTANCE PROGRAMS

SOCIAL INSURANCE TRANSFERS

Social Security Retirement

A non-means-tested program officially called Old Age, Survivors, and Dependent Insurance Program (OASDI). Provides monthly retirement benefits to covered workers or their surviving spouses and dependent children. It is the largest social insurance program. Since 1972, benefits have been indexed to rise with inflation.

Social Security Disability

A cash payment program that provides monthly benefits to covered workers who are disabled and their dependents.

Medicare

A federal health coverage program that covers partial (80 percent) medical costs for the elderly 65 years of age and older who are eligible for Social Security retirement. Provides coverage to people who are disabled if eligibility requirements are met.

Unemployment Insurance

A partial wage replacement program that provides up to 26 weeks of payments to covered workers who involuntarily lose their jobs.

Veterans Benefits

A federal program for veterans of all wars. Provides cash assistance for needy and disabled veterans, and survivors of veterans; veterans' education benefits; the Veterans Administrations hospital and medical care program; and veterans housing benefits.

MEANS-TESTED CASH ASSISTANCE TRANSFERS
Aid to Families with Dependent Children

>Direct grants to poor families with dependent children under 18. Due to the passage of the Family Support Act of 1988, this program now covers both one-parent and two-parent families.

Supplemental Security Income

>A totally federalized program that provides direct grants to the needy aged, disabled, and blind. Like Social Security, benefits are indexed to rise with inflation.

MEANS-TESTED NONCASH TRANSFERS
Medicaid

>A health care program that is regulated by the states to cover most medical costs for the poor. AFDC and SSI recipients are automatically eligible.

Food Stamps

>A food coupon program that enables families with incomes below 130 percent of the poverty line to purchase additional food items each month.

Public and Subsidized Housing

>A housing program that provides low-rent public housing and rent supplements to elderly and low-income families.

School Lunch Program

>A nutrition program that provides reduced-price lunches to all students in participating schools.

INDEX

Abramovitz, Mimi 8, 27, 50, 51, 64, 66
Act of Settlement 18
ADC 25-31, 33
Addams, Jane 21, 22
Aid to Families with Dependent Children (AFDC) 2, 16, 18, 56
black families 43
black female-headed households 62
Bureau of Labor Statistics 68
capitalism 1, 2, 7-10, 14, 29, 43, 48, 60, 63, 69
capitalist patriarchy 3, 8, 12-16
Carter, Jimmy 67
cash assistance transfers 57
Charity Organization Society 19, 30
charity workers 22
child care 2, 12, 31, 62-65, 68, 69, 71-74, 77
child support 47, 63
child-care tax credit 70
childbearing 5, 6, 68
childrearing 5, 6, 23, 68
children's allowances 71, 72
Children's Defense Fund 73
Civil Rights Act of 1964 15
Civilian Works Administration (CWA) 26
class..... 1, 3-8, 11-14, 18, 20-22, 27, 31, 38, 39. 48-50, 52, 58, 69,
                                                    74, 76-78
Committee on Economic Security 24-26
comparable worth 4, 11, 34, 65, 67, 68, 74, 78
Compensatory Education Aid 57
conservatives 33, 34, 50, 52, 60
Consumer Price Index 39, 59
Danziger, Sheldon 58, 70, 72
Department of Agriculture 39
Department of Health and Human Services 57, 73
dependent children........2, 3, 10, 16, 18, 22, 25-28, 31, 32, 43, 47,
                              53, 56, 57, 59. 61, 62, 65, 70, 75
Depression 17, 23-25, 29. 48, 49, 65, 74, 77
disabled 18, 34. 35, 48, 53, 59, 66
discrimination 3, 11, 12. 15, 26, 31, 38, 67

93

Dix, Dorothea 20
earned income tax credit (EITC) 70
Economic Opportunity Act 32, 39
Economy Food Plan 39
Eisenhower Administration 28
elderly 1, 18, 27, 35, 45, 48, 53, 59, 75
Elizabethan Poor Laws 17
Employment & Job Training 57
empowerment 77
Engels, Friedrich 14, 21
entitlement programs 35, 51
Equal Employment Opportunity Commission 67
Equal Pay Act of 1963 15
Equal Rights Amendment 2
eugenics 20, 21
exchange value 7, 14
family 2, 4-6, 8-11, 14, 16, 1 7, 21, 22, 27, 30-34, 36, 38, 39,
            43, 46, 47, 50, 51, 59, 60, 62, 64, 65, 68-72, 77, 78
Family Assistance Plan 34
family policy 68, 71, 72
family wage 9
female-headed families 2, 30, 43, 47, 61, 62
female-headed households 30, 31, 38, 43, 47, 62
feminist theory 1, 4, 5, 8
feminists 4-6, 8, 13, 16, 21, 77-79
feminization of poverty 2, 3, 15, 37, 38, 43
Food Stamps 39, 49, 56, 57, 59, 61
Freud, Sigmund 24
full employment 62, 65-67, 74, 78
Full Employment Bill of 1945 65
gender 4, 5, 8, 9, 11, 12, 15, 38, 39, 43, 50, 58, 59, 61, 65,
                                              69, 74, 76-78
Hartley, Robert 20
Hawkins-Reuss Bill 66
Head Start 73
health care 22, 62, 64, 65, 73-77, 79
Hispanic families 43
homeless 1, 37, 71
household labor 3, 7, 9, 11, 13, 18, 65, 69
housework 5, 7, 9-13, 51, 68, 69, 74

```
Hull House ....................................... 21
human resource programs .......................... 52-58
human resource spending ............................ 53
husbands ......................... 2, 9, 26, 30, 35, 38, 51
immigrants ................................... 21, 22
inequality ................... 1, 3, 4, 8, 15, 21, 28, 31, 38
inflation ......................... 35, 53, 59, 66, 67, 70
institutional services ............................... 51
jobs ...... 1, 2, 7, 12-15, 19, 23, 26, 27, 29, 31, 32, 34-36, 38, 50,
                                              62-68, 73, 75
Johnson, Lyndon B. ............................. 25, 32
Kennedy, John F. ............................... 29, 31
labor market ....1, 2, 4, 5, 7, 8, 12-15, 23, 24, 26, 27, 31, 34, 50, 51,
           56, 59, 62, 65, 66, 67, 68, 70, 73, 75, 79
labor unions .................................. 22, 26
Lanham Act ....................................... 72
liberal feminism ................................... 4-6
liberals ........................... 1, 33, 34, 50, 52, 60
lobbies .............................. 36, 58, 61, 74
local responsibility .......................... 18, 19, 52
Losing Ground ................................... 61
Lowell, Josephine Shaw ........................... 19, 20
man-in-the-house rules ............................. 30
marriage ........................... 5, 9, 33, 48, 59, 69
marriage laws ................................. 48, 59
Marx, Karl ......................... 5, 7, 14, 20, 21, 24
Marxism ................................. 6, 8, 21, 38
maternity leaves ................................... 47
means-tested income transfers ...................... 56, 57
means-tested programs ........................... 36, 49
Medicaid .................. 31, 39, 49, 56, 57, 61, 74, 76
Medicare ............. 35, 36, 45, 49, 52-54, 56-58, 74, 76
midnight raids .................................... 30
minimum income guarantee ..................... 69, 71, 74
minimum wage ........................... 31, 64, 67, 72
minorities ....................... 11, 22, 28, 49, 60, 65
motherhood ..................................... 9, 11
mothers' pensions ............................ 22, 23, 25
Moynihan, Daniel P. ........................... 34, 62-64
Murray, Charles ................................. 61, 62
```

National Coalition on Women, Work and Welfare Reform . . 62, 64
national health care 65, 74, 76, 77
National Recovery Administration (NRA) 26
New Deal 24, 26, 48, 74
Nixon, Richard M. 34
Norton, Eleanor Holmes 67
nuclear family 8-10
Omnibus Budget Reconciliation Act 36
Omnibus Welfare Reform Bill 34
oppression 4-6, 8, 13-16, 38, 52, 58
parents' wages 65, 68, 69, 72, 74
patriarchy 1, 3, 6, 8-10, 12-16, 38
Perkins, Frances 24
Phillips Curve 66
poor children 45, 46, 73
poverty 1-3, 6, 15, 16, 19-21, 24, 26-33, 35-48, 56, 59, 61, 63-67,
70-72, 75, 78
poverty index 39
poverty level 2, 35, 36, 39-41, 43, 44, 46, 56, 59, 75
poverty rate 16, 30, 39, 40, 43-46
poverty threshold 38, 39, 47, 64
primary labor market 34
productive labor 2, 7, 11, 69
progressive feminist social welfare agenda . . 47, 52, 65, 69, 77, 79
Public & Subsidized Housing 57
public assistances 24
public welfare 2, 15, 28-31, 38, 50
race 5, 20, 39, 41, 42, 46, 58, 69, 74, 76-78
racism 6, 24, 38
radical feminism 5, 6, 8
Reagan, Ronald 35-37, 39, 49, 53, 58, 61, 63
Reaganomics 35, 37
residency requirements 19, 22
residual services 51
Roosevelt, Franklin Delano 24
Roosevelt, Theodore 22
School Lunch Programs 56, 57
secondary labor market 12, 15, 31, 50, 62, 65, 67, 75
settlement workers 21, 22
sexism 4, 8, 16, 24

sexual discrimination 15, 31
sexual division of labor 5, 8, 9, 11, 13, 14, 16, 31, 62, 64
single mothers 43, 45, 48, 50, 53, 58, 59
social change 1, 4, 22, 77, 79
Social Darwinism 19
social insurance transfers 56, 57
social insurances 24, 25, 58
social reform 21
Social Security 10, 24-26, 29, 31, 33-36, 39, 45, 48-53, 56-59,
63, 72, 74
Social Security Act 24
Social Security Administration 29, 34, 39, 57
social welfare institution 24, 49
social welfare policy 2, 10, 16, 17, 19, 20, 23, 24, 28, 29, 31,
35, 45, 47-52, 60, 66, 68, 70
social welfare system 1, 17, 48-50, 77
social work 21-24, 29, 70
socialism 21
socialist feminism 4, 6, 8, 9, 13, 15
socialization 3-6, 12, 14, 15, 60
Supplemental Security Income (SSI) 56, 59
Supreme Court 19, 20, 30, 51
surplus value 7, 69
tax reform 65, 69, 70, 72, 78
The Communist Manifesto 21
U.S. Bureau of the Census 16, 31, 38-42, 44-46
underemployment 1-3, 47
unemployment . 1-3, 24, 25, 27, 28, 38, 47-49, 56-58, 61, 55-67, 72
Unemployment Insurance 24, 49, 56-58, 61
universal child care 59, 72-74
universal health care 74, 76
unproductive labor 7
use value 7, 14
veterans 49, 55-58
Veterans' Benefits 49, 56-58
wages 2, 7, 9, 11, 12, 19, 21, 25, 26, 28, 38 43, 51, 62, 64-69,
72, 74, 75
War on Poverty 32, 39, 56, 61, 63
welfare 1, 2, 10, 13, 15-20, 22-38, 43, 45, 47-53, 56, 58-66,
68-71, 74, 76, 77, 78-79

welfare reform 33, 34, 61-64, 71, 78
welfare state 13, 15, 17, 29, 49, 56, 58, 60, 61, 77
White House Conference on Children 22
widows 23, 26, 33, 50
wives 9, 26, 28, 51
work ethic 17, 18, 36
Work Incentive Program (WIN) 33, 63
work programs 63
workfare 19, 63
Works Progress Administration (WPA) 26
World War II 27, 65, 72